Microsoft®
MCSE
Readiness Review

Exam 70-098
Implementing and Supporting
Microsoft Windows® 98

Microsoft Press

PUBLISHED BY
Microsoft Press
A Division of Microsoft Corporation
One Microsoft Way
Redmond, Washington 98052-6399

Copyright © 1999 by Dave Perkovich

Library of Congress Cataloging-in-Publication Data
Perkovich, Dave.
     MCSE Readiness Review : Exam 70-098, Implementing and Supporting
Microsoft Windows 98 / Dave Perkovich.
         p. cm.
     Includes index.
     ISBN 0-7356-0671-4
     1. Electronic data processing personnel--Certification.
     2. Microsoft software--Examinations--Study guides.   3. Microsoft
Windows (Computer file)   I. Title.
QA76.3.P473   1999
005.4'469--dc21   99-10772
                                                                           CIP

Printed and bound in the United States of America.

1 2 3 4 5 6 7 8 9   MLML   4 3 2 1 0 9

Distributed in Canada by ITP Nelson, a division of Thomson Canada Limited.

A CIP catalogue record for this book is available from the British Library.

Microsoft Press books are available through booksellers and distributors worldwide. For further information about international editions, contact your local Microsoft Corporation office or contact Microsoft Press International directly at fax (425) 936-7329. Visit our Web site at mspress.microsoft.com.

Acquisitions Editor: Jeff Madden
Project Editor: Lynn Finnel

Contents

Welcome to Implementing and Supporting Microsoft Windows 98

Welcome to *MCSE Readiness Review—Exam 70-098: Implementing and Supporting Microsoft Windows 98*. The Readiness Review series gives you a focused, time-saving way to identify the information you need to know to pass the Microsoft Certified Professional (MCP) exams. The series combines a realistic electronic assessment with a review book to help you become familiar with the types of questions you will encounter on the MCP exam. By reviewing the objectives and sample questions, you can focus on the specific skills that you need to improve before taking the exam.

This book helps you evaluate your readiness for the MCP Exam 70-098: Implementing and Supporting Microsoft Windows 98. When you pass this exam, you achieve Microsoft Certified Professional status. You also earn core credit toward the Microsoft Certified Systems Engineer (MCSE) certification and core credit toward the Microsoft Certified Systems Engineer + Internet certification.

Note You can find a complete list of MCP exams and their related objectives on the Microsoft Certified Professional Web site at http://www.microsoft.com/mcp.

The Readiness Review series lets you identify any areas in which you may need additional training. To help you get the training you need to successfully pass the certification exams, Microsoft Press publishes a complete line of self-paced training kits and other study materials. For comprehensive information about the topics covered in the Windows 98 exam, you might want to see the corresponding training kit—*Windows 98*.

Before You Begin

This MCSE Readiness Review consists of two main parts: the Readiness Review electronic assessment on the accompanying compact disc, and this Readiness Review book.

The Readiness Review Components

The electronic assessment is a practice certification exam that helps you evaluate your skills. It provides instant scoring feedback, so you can determine areas in which additional study may be helpful before you take the certification exam. Although your score on the electronic assessment does not necessarily indicate what your score will be on the certification exam, it does give you the opportunity to answer questions that are similar to those on the actual certification exam.

The Readiness Review book is organized by the exam's objectives. Each chapter of the book pertains to one of the six primary groups of objectives on the actual exam, called the *Objective Domains*. Each Objective Domain lists the tested skills you need to master to adequately answer the exam questions. Because the certification exams focus on real-world skills, the Tested Skills and Suggested Practices lists provide suggested practices that emphasize the practical application of the exam objectives.

Within each Objective Domain, you will find the related objectives that are covered on the exam. Each objective provides you with the following:

- Key terms you must know in order to understand the objective. Knowing these terms can help you answer the objective's questions correctly.

- Several sample exam questions with the correct answers. The answers are accompanied by discussions as to why each answer is correct or incorrect. (These questions match the questions you find on the electronic assessment.)

- Suggestions for further reading or additional resources to help you understand the objective and increase your ability to perform the tasks or skills specified by the objective.

You use the electronic assessment to determine the exam objectives that you need to study, and then use the Readiness Review book to learn more about those particular objectives and discover additional study materials to supplement your knowledge. You can also use the Readiness Review book to research the answers to specific sample test questions. Keep in mind that to pass the exam, you should understand not only the answer to the question, but also the concepts upon which the correct answer is based.

MCP Exam Prerequisites

In addition to your hands-on experience working with Windows 98, you should have a working knowledge of the following procedures:

- Using an operating system with a graphical user interface, such as Microsoft Windows 95, Microsoft Windows 98, or Microsoft Windows NT 4.0

- Installing application software

- Installing hardware, such as memory, communication peripherals, and disk drives

- Being familiar with software files including batch files, AUTOEXEC.BAT files, and CONFIG.SYS files

---

Note After you have used the Readiness Review and determined that you are ready for the exam, see the "Test Registration and Fees" section in the Appendix for information on scheduling for the exam. You can schedule exams up to six weeks in advance, or as late as one working day before the exam date.

Know the Products

Microsoft's certification program relies on exams that measure your ability to perform a specific job function or set of tasks. Microsoft develops the exams by analyzing the tasks performed by people who are currently performing the job function. Therefore, the specific knowledge, skills, and abilities relating to the job are reflected in the certification exam.

Because the certification exams are based on real-world tasks, you need to gain hands-on experience with the applicable technology in order to master the exam. In a sense, you might consider hands-on experience in an organizational environment to be a prerequisite for passing an MCP exam. Many of the questions relate directly to Microsoft products or technology, so use opportunities at your organization or home to practice using the relevant tools.

Using the MCSE Readiness Review

Although you can use the Readiness Review in a number of ways, you might start your studies by taking the electronic assessment as a pretest. After completing the exam, review your results for each Objective Domain and focus your studies first on the Objective Domains where you received the lowest scores. The electronic assessment allows you to print your results, and a printed report of how you fared can be useful when reviewing the exam material in this book.

After you have taken the Readiness Review electronic assessment, use the Readiness Review book to learn more about the Objective Domains that you find difficult and to find listings of appropriate study materials that may supplement your knowledge. By reviewing why the answers are correct or incorrect, you can determine if you made a simple comprehension error or if you need to study the objective topics more.

Alternatively, you can use the Learn Now feature of the electronic assessment to review your answer to each question. This feature provides you with the correct answer and a reference to the *Windows 98 Training* kit (purchased separately) or other resources. If you use this method and you need additional information to understand an answer, you can also reference the question in the Readiness Review book.

You can also use the Readiness Review book to focus on the exact objectives that you need to master. Each objective in the book contains several questions that help you determine if you understand the information related to that particular skill. The book is also designed for you to answer each question before turning the page to review the correct answer.

The best method to prepare for the MCP exam is to use the Readiness Review book in conjunction with the electronic assessment and other study material. Thoroughly studying and practicing the material combined with substantial real-world experience can help you fully prepare for the MCP exam.

Understanding the Readiness Review Conventions

Before you start using the Readiness Review, it is important that you understand the terms and conventions used in the electronic assessment and book.

Question Numbering System

The Readiness Review electronic assessment and book contain reference numbers for each question. Understanding the numbering format will help you use the Readiness Review more effectively. When Microsoft creates the exams, the questions are grouped by job skills called *objectives*. These objectives are then organized by sections known as *Objective Domains*. Each question can be identified by the Objective Domain and the objective it covers. The question numbers follow this format:

Test Number.Objective Domain.Objective.Question Number

For example, question number 70-098.02.01.003 means this is question three (003) for the first objective (01) in the second Objective Domain (02) of the Windows 98 exam (70-098). Refer to the "Exam Objectives Summary" section later in this introduction to locate the numbers associated with particular objectives. Each question is numbered based on its presentation in the printed book. You can use this numbering system to reference questions on the electronic assessment or in the Readiness Review book. Even though the questions in the book are organized by objective, you will see questions in random order during the electronic assessment and actual certification exam.

Notational Conventions

- Characters or commands that you type appear in **bold lowercase** type.

- Variable information is *italicized. Italic* is also used to identify new terms and book titles.

- Acronyms appear in FULL CAPITALS.

Notes

Notes appear throughout the book.

- Notes marked **Note** contain supplemental information.

- Notes marked **Caution** contain information you will want to know before continuing with the book's material.

Using the Readiness Review Electronic Assessment

The Readiness Review electronic assessment is designed to provide you with an experience that simulates that of the actual MCP exam. The electronic assessment material mirrors the type and nature of the questions you will see on the certification exam. Furthermore, the electronic assessment format approximates the certification exam format and includes additional features to help you prepare for the real examination.

Each iteration of the electronic assessment consists of 60 questions covering all the objectives for the Windows 98 exam. (The actual certification exams generally consist of 50 to 70 questions, although fewer questions are presented if you are taking a computer adaptive test.) Just like a real certification exam, you see questions from the objectives in random order during the practice test. Similar to the certification exam, the electronic assessment allows you to mark questions and review them after you finish the test.

Note For more information about computer adaptive testing, refer to the "Computer Adaptive Testing" section in the Appendix.

To increase its value as a study aid, you can take the electronic assessment multiple times. Each time you are presented with a different set of questions in a revised order; however, some questions may be repeated from exams you may have taken earlier.

If you have used one of the certification exam preparation tests available from Microsoft, the Readiness Review electronic assessment should look familiar. The difference is that the electronic assessment covers more questions while providing you with the opportunity to learn as you take the exam.

Installing and Running the Electronic Assessment Software

Before you begin using the electronic assessment, you need to install the software. You need a computer with the following minimum configuration:

- 486 or higher Intel-based processor (486 must be running in Enhanced Mode)

- Microsoft Windows 95 or later (including Windows NT)

- 4 MB of RAM

- 15 MB of available disk space

- CD-ROM drive

- Mouse or other pointing device (recommended)

▶ **To install the electronic assessment**

1. Insert the Readiness Review compact disc into your CD-ROM drive.

2. From the root directory of the compact disc, open the Assess folder and double-click the Setup.exe file.

   A dialog box appears indicating you will install the MCSE Readiness Review test.

3. Click Next.

   The Select Destination Directory dialog box appears showing a default installation directory (named C:\MP098, where C: is the name assigned to your hard disk).

4. Either accept the default or change the installation directory if needed, and then click Next.

   The electronic assessment software installs.

Note These procedures describe using the electronic assessment on a computer running Windows 95, Windows 98, or Windows NT 4.0.

▶ **To start the electronic assessment**

1. From the Start menu, point to Programs, point to MCSE Readiness Review, and then click (70-098) Implementing and Supporting Windows 98.

   The electronic assessment program starts.

2. Click Start Test, or from the main menu, double-click the test name.

   Information about the MCSE Readiness Review series appears.

3. Click Start Test.

Taking the Electronic Assessment

The Readiness Review electronic assessment consists of 60 multiple-choice questions, and as in the certification exam, you can skip questions or mark them for later review. Each exam question contains a reference number that you can use to refer back to the Readiness Review book, and if you want, you can pause and continue taking the exam at a later time.

The electronic assessment contains simulation questions that use the same simulation software as the actual certification exam. These questions test your working knowledge of the software by requiring that you start the simulation and perform a specified task. After you complete the task, you close the simulator by clicking the close button in the upper-right corner of the simulation window, or by clicking the Next or Previous button.

Before you end the electronic assessment, you should make sure to answer all the questions. When the exam is graded, unanswered questions are counted as incorrect and will lower your score. Similarly, on the actual certification exam you should complete all questions or they will be counted as incorrect. No trick questions appear on the exam. The correct answer will always be among the list of choices. Some questions may require more than one response, and this will be indicated in the question. A good strategy is to eliminate the most obvious incorrect answers first to make it easier for you to select the correct answer.

You have 90 minutes to complete the electronic assessment. During the exam you will see a timer indicating the amount of time you have remaining. This will help you to gauge the amount of time you should use to answer each question and to complete the exam. The amount of time you are given on the actual certification exam varies with each exam. Generally, certification exams take approximately 90 minutes to complete.

During the electronic assessment, you can find the answer to each question by clicking the Learn Now button as you review the question. You see the correct answer and a reference to the applicable section of the *Microsoft Windows 98 Training* kit and other resources, which can be purchased separately.

Ending and Grading the Electronic Assessment

When you click the Grade Now button, you have the opportunity to review the questions you marked or left incomplete. This format is similar to the one used on the actual certification exam. When you are satisfied with your answers, click the Grade Test button. The electronic assessment is graded, and the software presents your section scores and your total score.

Note You can always end a test without grading your electronic assessment by clicking the Quit Test button.

After your electronic assessment is graded, you can view a list of Microsoft Press references by clicking the Review Incorrect Answers button. You can then click OK to view the questions you missed.

Interpreting the Electronic Assessment Results

The Section Scoring screen shows you the number of questions in each Objective Domain section, the number of questions you answered correctly, and a percentage grade for each section. You can use the Section Scoring screen to determine where to spend additional time studying. On the actual certification exam, the number of questions and passing score will depend on the exam you are taking. The electronic assessment records your score each time you grade an exam so you can track your progress over time.

▶ **To view your progress and exam records**

1. From the electronic assessment main menu, select File, then select History, and then choose View.

2. Click View History.

   Each attempt score and your total score appears.

3. Select an attempt, and then click View Details.

   The section score for each attempt appears. You can review the section score information to determine which Objective Domains you should study further. You can also use the scores to determine your progress as you continue to study and prepare for the real exam.

Ordering More Questions

Self Test Software offers practice tests to help you prepare for a variety of MCP certification exams. These practice tests contain hundreds of additional questions and are similar to the Readiness Review electronic assessment. For a fee, you can order exam practice tests for this exam and other Microsoft certification exams. Click on the To Order More Questions button on the electronic assessment main menu for more information.

Using the Readiness Review Book

You can use the Readiness Review book as a supplement to the Readiness Review electronic assessment, or as a stand-alone study aid. If you decide to use the book as a stand-alone study aid, review the Table of Contents or the list of objectives to find topics of interest or an appropriate starting point for you. To get the greatest benefit from the book, use the electronic assessment as a pretest to determine the Objective Domains where you should spend the most study time. Or, if you would like to research specific questions while taking the electronic assessment, you can use the question number located on the question screen to reference the question number in the Readiness Review book.

One way to determine areas where additional study may be helpful is to carefully review your individual section scores from the electronic assessment and note objective areas where your score could be improved. The section scores correlate to the Objective Domains listed in the Readiness Review book.

Reviewing the Objectives

Each Objective Domain in the book contains an introduction and a list of practice skills. Each list of practice skills describes suggested tasks you can perform to help you understand the objectives. Some of the tasks suggest reading additional material, while others are hands-on practices with software or hardware. You should pay particular attention to the hands-on suggestions, as the certification exam reflects real-world knowledge you can gain only by working with the software or technology. Increasing your real-world experience with the relevant products and technologies will greatly enhance your performance on the exam.

Once you have determined the objectives you would like to study, you can use the Table of Contents to locate the objectives in the Readiness Review book. When reviewing a specific objective, you should make sure you understand the purpose of the objective and the skill or knowledge it is measuring on the certification exam. You can study each objective separately, but you may need to understand the concepts explained in other objectives.

Make sure you understand the key terms for each objective. You will need a thorough understanding of these terms to answer the objective's questions correctly. Key term definitions are located in the Glossary of this book.

Reviewing the Questions

Each odd-numbered page contains one or two questions followed by the possible answers. After you review the question and select a probable answer, you can turn to the following page to determine if you answered the question correctly. (For information about the question numbering format, see "Question Numbering System," earlier in this introduction.)

The Readiness Review briefly discusses each possible answer and provides a specific reason why each answer is correct or incorrect. You should review the discussion of each possible answer to help you understand why the correct answer is the best answer among the choices given. You should understand not only the answer to the question, but the concepts on which the correct answer is based. If you feel you need more information about a topic or you do not understand the answer, use the Further Reading section in each objective to learn where you can find more information.

The answers to the questions in the Readiness Review are based on current industry specifications and standards. However, the information provided by the answers is subject to change as technology improves and changes.

Exam Objectives Summary

This Windows 98 certification (70-098) exam measures your ability to implement, administer, and troubleshoot information systems that incorporate Microsoft Windows 98 and measures your ability to provide technical support to users of Windows 98. Before taking the exam, you should be proficient with the job skills presented in the following sections. The sections provide the exam objectives and the corresponding objective numbers (which you can use to reference the questions in the Readiness Review electronic assessment and book) grouped by Objective Domains.

Objective Domain 1: Planning

The objectives in Objective Domain 1 are as follows:

- Objective 1.1 (70-098.01.01)—Develop an appropriate implementation model for specific requirements in a Microsoft environment and a mixed Microsoft and NetWare environment.

- Objective 1.2 (70-098.01.02)—Develop a security strategy in a Microsoft environment and a mixed Microsoft and NetWare environment.

Objective Domain 2: Installation and Configuration

The objectives in Objective Domain 2 are as follows:

- Objective 2.1 (70-098.02.01)—Install Windows 98.

- Objective 2.2 (70-098.02.02)—Configure Windows 98 Server Components.

- Objective 2.3 (70-098.02.03)—Install and configure the network components of Windows 98 in a Microsoft environment and a mixed Microsoft and NetWare environment.

- Objective 2.4 (70-098.02.04)—Install and configure network protocols in a Microsoft environment and a mixed Microsoft and NetWare environment.

- Objective 2.5 (70-098.02.05)—Install and configure hardware devices in a Microsoft environment and a mixed Microsoft and NetWare environment.

- Objective 2.6 (70-098.02.06)—Install and configure Microsoft Backup.

Objective Domain 3: Configuring and Managing Resource Access

The objectives in Objective Domain 3 are as follows:

- Objective 3.1 (70-098.03.01)—Assign access permissions for shared folders in a Microsoft environment and a mixed Microsoft and NetWare environment.

- Objective 3.2 (70-098.03.02)—Create, share, and monitor resources including remote computers and network printers.

- Objective 3.3 (70-098.03.03)—Set up user environments by using user profiles and system policies.

- Objective 3.4 (70-098.03.04)—Back up data and restore data.

- Objective 3.5 (70-098.03.05)—Configure hard disks.

- Objective 3.6 (70-098.03.06)—Create hardware profiles.

Objective Domain 4: Integration and Interoperability

The objectives in Objective Domain 4 are as follows:

- Objective 4.1 (70-098.04.01)—Configure a Windows 98 computer as a client computer in a Windows NT network.

- Objective 4.2 (70-098.04.02)—Configure a Windows 98 computer as a client computer in a NetWare network.

- Objective 4.3 (70-098.04.03)—Configure a Windows 98 computer for remote access.

Objective Domain 5: Monitoring and Optimization

The objectives in Objective Domain 5 are as follows:

- Objective 5.1 (70-098.05.01)—Monitor system performance.

- Objective 5.2 (70-098.05.02)—Tune and optimize the system in a Microsoft environment and a mixed Microsoft and NetWare environment.

Objective Domain 6:Troubleshooting

The objectives in Objective Domain 6 are as follows:

- Objective 6.1 (70-098.06.01)—Diagnose and resolve installation failures.

- Objective 6.2 (70-098.06.02)—Diagnose and resolve boot process failures.

- Objective 6.3 (70-098.06.03)—Diagnose and resolve connectivity problems in a Microsoft environment and a mixed Microsoft and NetWare environment.

- Objective 6.4 (70-098.06.04)—Diagnose and resolve printing problems in a Microsoft environment and a mixed Microsoft and NetWare environment.

- Objective 6.5 (70-098.06.05)—Diagnose and resolve file system problems.

- Objective 6.6 (70-098.06.06)—Diagnose and resolve resource access problems in a Microsoft environment and a mixed Microsoft and NetWare environment.

- Objective 6.7 (70-098.06.07)—Diagnose and resolve hardware device and device driver problems.

Getting More Help

A variety of resources are available to help you study for the exam. Your options include instructor-led classes, seminars, self-paced kits, or other learning materials. The materials described here are created to prepare you for MCP exams. Each training resource fits a different type of learning style and budget.

Microsoft Official Curriculum (MOC)

Microsoft Official Curriculum (MOC) courses are technical training courses developed by Microsoft product groups to educate computer professionals who use Microsoft technology. The courses are developed with the same objectives used for Microsoft certification, and MOC courses are available to support most exams for the MCSE certification. The courses are available in instructor-led, online, or self-paced formats to fit your preferred learning style.

Self-Paced Training

Microsoft Press self-paced training kits cover a variety of Microsoft technical products. The self-paced kits, which are based on MOC courses, feature self-paced lessons, hands-on practices, multimedia presentations, practice files, and demonstration software. They can help you understand the concepts and get the experience you need to prepare for the corresponding MCP exam. To help you prepare for the Implementing and Supporting Windows 98 (70-098) MCP exam, Microsoft has written the *Windows 98 Training* kit. With this official self-paced training kit, you can learn the skills and knowledge required to install, configure, support, and troubleshoot Microsoft Windows 98 in both stand-alone and networked environments. This kit gives you training for the real world by offering hands-on training through CD-ROM-based exercises.

MCP Approved Study Guides

MCP Approved Study Guides, available through several organizations, are learning tools that help you prepare for MCP exams. The study guides are available in a variety of formats to match your learning style, including books, compact discs, online content, and videos. These guides come in a wide range of prices to fit your budget.

Microsoft Seminar Series

Microsoft Solution Providers and other organizations are often a source of information to help you prepare for an MCP exam. For example, many solution providers will present seminars to help industry professionals understand a particular product technology, such as networking. For information on all Microsoft-sponsored events, visit http://events.microsoft.com.

Planning

Windows 98 includes a number of features that can be implemented when connecting to a network. Both Windows NT and NetWare domains are supported. If neither server type is available, you can configure Windows 98 to run in a peer-to-peer workgroup network. When planning to use Windows 98 on a network, you will need to consider issues such as what levels of security and user management are required. What network protocols are used by other systems on the network? Will the Windows 98 computer share its files or printer with other computers on the network? What file system should be used? These and other questions must be answered before you can deploy Windows 98 and provide the users all the capabilities they require.

Tested Skills and Suggested Practices

The skills you need to successfully master the Planning Objective Domain on the exam include:

- **Implementing share-level and user-level security.**

  - Practice 1: Create a share on a folder that controls access based on share-level security. You do this by configuring a password on the share. Any user on the network who knows the password will be able to access the files in this folder.

  - Practice 2: With a Windows NT server on the network, add the Windows 98 computer to the domain, and configure a shared folder to use user-level security. You do this by allowing specific users or groups access to the files in the folder. The Windows NT server will provide a list of available users and groups.

- **Converting a FAT16 file system to FAT32.**

  - Practice 1: Install MS-DOS, or Windows 95, on a computer. By default the file system will be FAT16. Note the amount of space on the hard drive. Install Windows 98 and use the Drive Converter Wizard to convert the file system to

FAT32. Once the conversion has finished, note the new amount of space available on the drive. Since FAT32 uses smaller cluster sizes, you should see an increase of available space.

- **Implementing system policies.**

  - Practice 1: Use System Policy Editor to create a policy based on a user account. Log on to Windows 98 using this account to verify the settings.

  - Practice 2: With a Windows NT server available, create a system policy based on a group. Log on to Windows 98 with a user account that is in this group to verify the settings.

- **Implementing user profiles.**

  - Practice 1: Using Control Panel, enable unique user profiles. Log on to Windows 98 with two different user names to verify that the desktop configurations are maintained from one logon to another.

  - Practice 2: Configure the user profiles to support roaming users. This will require a Windows NT or NetWare server to store the user profile files.

- **Supporting Microsoft and NetWare network resources.**

  - Practice 1: Using the Network Neighborhood properties sheet, install Client for Microsoft Networks. Connect to a Windows NT Server resource to test the configuration.

  - Practice 2: Using the Network Neighborhood properties sheet, install Client for NetWare Networks. Connect to a NetWare server resource to test the configuration.

  - Practice 3: Install File and Printer Sharing for Microsoft Networks, and share a local printer. Connect to the Windows 98 computer from another system on the network, and test printing to the shared printer resource.

- **Logging on to a Windows NT domain.**

  - Practice 1: Configure Windows 98 to log on to an existing Windows NT Server domain.

  - Practice 2: Using two different user accounts that exist in a Windows NT domain, log on to Windows 98 and test using the accounts to access different network resources. Each account should be configured to have different access on the network. For example, the first user account should be able to access a network file share to which the other account has not been given access.

OBJECTIVE 1.1

Develop an appropriate implementation model for specific requirements in a Microsoft environment and a mixed Microsoft and NetWare environment.

Considerations for this objective include choosing the appropriate file system and planning a workgroup. Windows 98 offers support for both FAT16 and FAT32 file systems. You should implement and use FAT32 if you do not need to dual boot to Windows NT (workstation or server). FAT32 uses smaller clusters and is therefore more efficient, allowing you to store more data on a partition. In addition, FAT32 allows you to format partitions larger than 2 GB. If you are upgrading from MS-DOS or Windows 95, which use FAT16, and want to use FAT32, Windows 98 includes a conversion utility called the Drive Converter Wizard. However, this is a one-way operation; you cannot convert a FAT32 system to FAT16. Consider the following if you plan to implement FAT32:

- Do not use FAT32 on any partition that other operating systems will use, except Windows 95 OSR2.

- MS-DOS, Windows 3.x, the original release of Windows 95, and Windows NT clients can read FAT32 partitions shared across a network.

- If you dual boot between Windows 98 and another operating system, such as Windows NT 4.x, the drive C partition cannot be FAT32.

- You cannot compress FAT32 partitions.

- Windows 98 MS-DOS mode fully supports FAT32, so you can run most MS-DOS-mode games and applications from FAT32 partitions.

Windows 98 has a number of built-in features to support network environments. These include both Microsoft and NetWare networks. When planning for certification, you will need to learn about how to implement Windows 98 in a NetWare environment. The same features included in Windows 95 for network management are included in Windows 98. For example, you still use the Network Neighborhood properties to configure network interface cards (NICs) and the specific network protocols required. Windows 98 supports the following network protocols:

- NetBIOS Extended User Interface (NetBEUI)

- Transmission Control Protocol/Internet Protocol (TCP/IP)

- Internetwork Packet Exchange/Sequenced Packet Exchange (IPX/SPX)

- Data Link Control (DLC)

To successfully answer the questions for this objective, you need a firm understanding of several key terms. For definitions of these terms, refer to the Glossary in this book.

Key Terms

- Data Link Control (DLC)

- Domain

- File Allocation Table 16 (FAT16)

- File Allocation Table 32 (FAT32)

- Internetwork Packet Exchange/Sequenced Packet Exchange (IPX/SPX)

- NetBIOS Extended User Interface (NetBEUI)

- Network protocol

- Share-level security

- Transmission Control Protocol/Internet Protocol (TCP/IP)

- User-level security

- Workgroup

70-098.01.01.001

A corporation is upgrading 80 of its Windows 95 computers to Windows 98. Because the network administration has not controlled workgroup configuration in the past, there are currently 30 work-groups. When Windows 98 is installed, you want to control the number of choices a user can make for his workgroup.

What must be done to limit the number of workgroups a user can join?

A. Set up a batch file so that only an administrator can enter a computer's workgroup name.

B. Edit the SYSTEM.INI file in the shared Windows 98 directory and add the names of the authorized workgroups.

C. Nothing can be done unless the computers log on to a security provider (Windows NT Server 4.0, Novell NetWare 4.11, etc.).

D. Create a WRKGRP.INI file containing the authorized workgroup names. Copy this file to the location of the Windows 98 source files.

70-098.01.01.001

A corporation is upgrading 80 of its Windows 95 computers to Windows 98. Because the network administration has not controlled workgroup configuration in the past, there are currently 30 workgroups. When Windows 98 is installed, you want to control the number of choices a user can make for his workgroup.

What must be done to limit the number of workgroups a user can join?

▶ **Correct Answer: D**

   A. **Incorrect.** Windows 98 will use the existing WRKGRP.INI file to provide a list of available workgroups. Requiring an administrator to enter the workgroup name is not the most efficient solution.

   B. **Incorrect.** The SYSTEM.INI file is not used to restrict the available workgroups. Use the WRKGRP.INI file instead.

   C. **Incorrect.** Since workgroups are typically used when no security provider is available, Windows NT Server and Novell NetWare are not required to limit the available workgroup choices.

   D. **Correct.** Windows 98 will use entries in the WRKGRP.INI file to restrict the available workgroups a user can select.

70-098.01.01.002

A company is upgrading all nine of its Windows 3.11 computers to Windows 98. All users need to be able to access each other's files and printers, but security is very important. There are no other computers on the network and no plans to add any computers or other operating systems.

What is the best way to set up these computers?

A. Configure all computers in a single workgroup and implement user-level security.

B. Configure all computers in a single workgroup and implement share-level security.

C. Set up one of the Windows 98 computers as a domain controller and implement user-level security.

D. Set up one of the Windows 98 computers as a domain controller and implement share-level security.

E. Set up five of the computers in a workgroup named WORKGROUP and the other four computers in a domain named DOMAIN. Implement user-level security.

F. Set up five of the computers in a workgroup named WORKGROUP and the other four computers in a domain named DOMAIN. Implement share-level security.

70-098.01.01.003

In which instance would you recommend using FAT32?

A. A user needs to use compression.

B. A user is using a real-mode application.

C. A computer's hard disk drive is over 4 GB.

D. A computer dual boots with Windows NT Workstation 4.0.

E. A user's computer has a 2-GB hard drive with 50 MB of free disk space, and the user is considering reverting to Windows 95.

70-098.01.01.002

A company is upgrading all nine of its Windows 3.11 computers to Windows 98. All users need to be able to access each other's files and printers, but security is very important. There are no other computers on the network and no plans to add any computers or other operating systems.

What is the best way to set up these computers?

▶ **Correct Answer: B**

A. **Incorrect.** User-level security requires an authentication server, such as Windows NT. In this case, no computer is acting as a Windows NT server.

B. **Correct.** Since there is no ability to implement a Windows NT domain, this is the best way to allow the network to manage users accessing each other's resources.

C. **Incorrect.** Windows 98 cannot act as a domain controller. Only Windows NT Server can provide this service.

D. **Incorrect.** Windows 98 cannot act as a domain controller. Only Windows NT Server can provide this service.

E. **Incorrect.** No domain controller is available; therefore, only a workgroup solution is possible. In addition, Windows NT Server is required to create and manage a domain.

F. **Incorrect.** No domain controller is available; therefore, only a workgroup solution is possible. In addition, Windows NT Server is required to create and manage a domain.

70-098.01.01.003

In which instance would you recommend using FAT32?

▶ **Correct Answer: C**

A. **Incorrect.** Only FAT16 file systems can be compressed using DriveSpace3.

B. **Incorrect.** Real-mode applications run equally well on FAT16 or FAT32 file systems. This would not be a reason for upgrading the user to FAT32.

C. **Correct.** Since FAT32 manages hard drive space more efficiently, users with hard drives that are 512 MB, or larger, can obtain more storage space when using FAT32.

D. **Incorrect.** FAT32 is not supported by other operating systems and should not be used in a dual boot environment.

E. **Incorrect.** There is no conversion utility to return a FAT32 system to a FAT16 system. Unless the user runs Windows 95 OSR2, earlier versions of Windows 95 will not be compatible with the FAT32 file system.

70-098.01.01.004

You are developing an implementation plan for upgrading existing Windows 3.11 computers to Windows 98. Which commands must be removed from CONFIG.SYS to prevent any potential problems during Windows 98 setup? (Choose three.)

A. QEMM

B. HIMEM

C. EMM386

D. 386MAX

E. CMD640X

F. SMARTDRV

70-098.01.01.004

You are developing an implementation plan for upgrading existing Windows 3.11 computers to Windows 98. Which commands must be removed from CONFIG.SYS to prevent any potential problems during Windows 98 setup? (Choose three.)

▶ **Correct Answers: A, C, and D**

A. **Correct.** You must remove memory managers, such as QEMM, or antivirus software prior to running Windows 98 Setup.

B. **Incorrect.** Although memory managers can interfere with Setup, HIMEM.SYS will not affect Windows 98 Setup.

C. **Correct.** You must remove memory managers, such as EMM386, or antivirus software prior to running Windows 98 Setup.

D. **Correct.** You must remove memory managers, such as 386MAX, or antivirus software prior to running Windows 98 Setup.

E. **Incorrect.** Only memory managers and antivirus software must be disabled. IDE controller software should not affect Setup.

F. **Incorrect.** Only memory managers and antivirus software must be disabled. Disk-caching software should not affect Setup.

70-098.01.01.005

A network's workstations currently use Windows 95. Each of the five workstations has a different hardware configuration. The following table shows the five workstations' hardware configurations:

Workstation Name	CPU	Memory	Hard Disk Space
Client_01	486DX33	24 MB	400 MB
Client_02	Pentium	12 MB	225 MB
Client_03	Pentium	32 MB	100 MB
Client_04	486DX66	16 MB	300 MB
Client_05	Pentium	64 MB	175 MB

Which computers can be upgraded to Windows 98 without upgrading hardware? (Choose all that apply.)

A. Client_01

B. Client_02

C. Client_03

D. Client_04

E. Client_05

70-098.01.01.005

A network's workstations currently use Windows 95. Each of the five workstations has a different hardware configuration. The following table shows the five workstations' hardware configurations:

Workstation Name	CPU	Memory	Hard Disk Space
Client_01	486DX33	24 MB	400 MB
Client_02	Pentium	12 MB	225 MB
Client_03	Pentium	32 MB	100 MB
Client_04	486DX66	16 MB	300 MB
Client_05	Pentium	64 MB	175 MB

Which computers can be upgraded to Windows 98 without upgrading hardware? (Choose all that apply.)

► **Correct Answers: D and E**

A. **Incorrect.** Windows 98 requires at least a 486DX66 processor.

B. **Incorrect.** Windows 98 requires at least 16 MB of RAM.

C. **Incorrect.** Windows 98 requires at least 175 MB of available drive space when using FAT32 (225 MB when using FAT16).

D. **Correct.** This system can run Windows 98 with its current hardware configuration.

E. **Correct.** This system can run Windows 98 with its current hardware configuration.

Further Reading

Microsoft Windows 98 Training Kit. Complete Lesson 2, "Choosing a File System in Windows 98," of Chapter 3, "Windows 98 File System Support." In this lesson, you will learn about the difference between FAT16 and FAT32.

Microsoft Windows 98 Training Kit. Complete Lesson 1, "Installing and Configuring Network Components," of Chapter 12, "Configuring Windows 98 for Use on a Network." In this lesson, you will learn how to configure different network protocols, such as TCP/IP, and support other network components within Windows 98.

Microsoft Windows 98 Resource Kit. Read pages 398–401 to learn more about the details and benefits of FAT32.

Windows 98 Accelerated MCSE Study Guide. Read Chapter 2, "Windows 98 Architecture," to learn more about the various file systems supported by Microsoft operating systems.

O B J E C T I V E   1 . 2

Develop a security strategy in a Microsoft environment and a mixed Microsoft and NetWare environment.

Strategies for this objective include system policies, user profiles, file and printer sharing, share-level access control, or user-level access control. Whether in a stand-alone environment, or while connected to Windows NT or NetWare networks, Windows 98 supports a variety of security implementations. By using system policies, administrators can control what the environment provides the user. This allows you to tighten access to both the system and the network. These configurations can be controlled by user, group, or computer and are created and managed using System Policy Editor. System Policy Editor will create registry settings on the system that override previous settings. These new settings are implemented when the user logs on based on his user name. This information is stored in the *.POL file, usually named CONFIG.POL.

In addition to system policies, specific user profiles can be implemented to customize the user's desktop environment. This configuration information is saved in the USER.DAT file, which is part of the Windows 98 registry. User profiles also allow for roaming users to maintain their settings from one computer to another. Both system policies and user profiles can be implemented together for virtually complete control over what is presented to the user and how.

To share local files or printers, Windows 98 must have the appropriate file and printer sharing installed depending on the network environment. Windows 98 includes these clients for both Microsoft and NetWare networks. Once the specific file and printer sharing client has been installed, you must then specifically turn on file and/or printer sharing. The fact that the client is installed does not mean that you can immediately start sharing resources. This also allows you to support one or the other. For instance, you may want to share your printer, but keep your local files secure.

Depending on whether a Windows NT or NetWare server is available to manage users, you may need to implement a workgroup environment. When using a workgroup environment, sometimes called a peer-to-peer network, you will only be able to use share-level access control to network resources. Share-level access allows you to control access based on a password. Unlike user-level access, share-level access means that any user who knows the resource's password will be able to access that resource. If you need to implement a more secured environment, namely one that controls access based on user name, you must implement user-level access and have a server available to manage the user accounts. When a user logs on to the Windows NT or NetWare domain, his account is validated. The user can then begin accessing the resources that he has been given permission to.

To successfully answer the questions for this objective, you need a firm understanding of several key terms. For definitions of these terms, refer to the Glossary in this book.

Key Terms

- Distributed file system (DFS)

- Primary Domain Controller (PDC)

- Roaming users

- System policies

- User profiles

70-098.01.02.001

A high school's Windows NT network has a single Windows NT Server 4.0 computer and 30 Windows 98 workstations. Multiple students use the Windows 98 workstations. Each student has different lab assignments.

You want to achieve these results:

- Allow certain students access to all the Windows 98 tools.
- Restrict the rest of the students from certain Windows 98 tools.
- Implement system policies.

Which steps must be performed to provide these results? (Choose three.)

A. Install group policy support on all the workstations.

B. Store the system policy files in the Netlogon share of the Primary Domain Controller (PDC).

C. Create groups that represent the different lab assignments using System Policy Editor.

D. Using System Policy Editor, create a user profile on the Windows NT server before assigning each user to a group.

E. Create groups that represent the different lab assignments on the Windows NT domain's PDC, assign permissions to the groups, and add the appropriate users to each group.

70-098.01.02.001

A high school's Windows NT network has a single Windows NT Server 4.0 computer and 30 Windows 98 workstations. Multiple students use the Windows 98 workstations. Each student has different lab assignments.

You want to achieve these results:

- Allow certain students access to all the Windows 98 tools.
- Restrict the rest of the students from certain Windows 98 tools.
- Implement system policies.

Which steps must be performed to provide these results? (Choose three.)

▶ Correct Answers: A, C, and E

A. **Correct.** Installing group policy support will be required to achieve the desired environment.

B. **Incorrect.** Unless multiple users will have access to the same machine, and centralized management is not desired, system policy files should be stored in the Netlogon directory of a Windows NT server. Windows 98 checks this location by default when the user logs on.

C. **Correct.** Although groups should be created based on the lab assignments, System Policy Editor is not the correct utility.

D. **Incorrect.** If a specific user policy exists, Windows 98 will ignore any group policies.

E. **Correct.** The users will need to be added to the specific groups based on the different lab assignments.

70-098.01.02.002

Three users share a computer. Each time they log on to the computer, they have to change their desktop settings. What is the easiest way to allow users to save their desktop configurations?

A. Set up local user profiles.

B. Set up roaming user profiles.

C. Set up a default user profile with which every user agrees.

D. Set up a Windows NT domain and implement mandatory profiles.

70-098.01.02.003

A Windows NT domain has 25 Windows 98 workstations. Each workstation is used by several different people in any given day. The users would like to maintain their personal desktop settings at the computers they use. What is the best way to accomplish this?

A. Create local user profiles for every user on the network's primary domain controller.

B. Create a roaming user profile for every user on the network's primary domain controller.

C. Instruct each user to create a desktop, and save the USER.DAT file to the Netlogon directory of the primary domain controller.

D. Instruct each user to create a desktop, and save the USER.DAT file to the <Windir> directory of each user's Windows 98 workstation.

70-098.01.02.002

Three users share a computer. Each time they log on to the computer, they have to change their desktop settings. What is the easiest way to allow users to save their desktop configurations?

▶ **Correct Answer: A**

A. **Correct.** Local user profiles will allow each user to configure the system based on his logon. No other resources (that is, servers) are required.

B. **Incorrect.** Roaming user profiles may solve this problem but are more complicated than using local user profiles in this scenario.

C. **Incorrect.** A default profile would not allow individual customization, which Windows 98 does support.

D. **Incorrect.** Implementing a Windows NT server would not be the most efficient solution to this problem.

70-098.01.02.003

A Windows NT domain has 25 Windows 98 workstations. Each workstation is used by several different people in any given day. The users would like to maintain their personal desktop settings at the computers they use. What is the best way to accomplish this?

▶ **Correct Answer: B**

A. **Incorrect.** Local user profiles should be created on the client machines and would not be the best solution in this environment.

B. **Correct.** Roaming user profiles would be the best solution since there are more users than computers in this environment.

C. **Incorrect.** Saving the USER.DAT file to the Netlogon directory will not allow the user to log on to other computers in the network.

D. **Incorrect.** Saving the USER.DAT file to the local <Windir> folder will not provide users the ability to log on to other computers in this environment and retain their settings.

70-098.01.02.004

You are upgrading all Windows 95 workstations on a company's Windows NT domain to Windows 98. The PDC is using Windows NT Server 4.0 and has support for DFS resources. How can DFS resources be accessed from the Windows 98 workstations? (Choose two.)

A. Windows 98 workstations must use SMB-based resources.

B. Windows 98 workstations can access DFS resources on NetWare 4.x servers.

C. Windows 98 workstations need to be upgraded with the DFS client support package.

D. Windows 98 workstations can access DFS resources from multiple locations using a single path.

70-098.01.02.005

All network workstations use Windows 98 as their only operating system. The workstations need to access all of the network's resources. There are five Windows NT Server 4.0 servers, three NetWare 3.1 servers, and two NetWare 4.11 servers using NDS.

What must be installed on the network's workstations to access resources located on all servers? (Choose all that apply.)

A. Install the IPX/SPX-compatible protocol to access both NetWare servers.

B. Install any additional protocol necessary to access the Windows NT 4.0 server.

C. Install the Client for Microsoft Networks to access resources on the Windows NT 4.0 server.

D. Install the Microsoft Client for NetWare Networks to access resources on the NetWare 3.x server.

E. Install the Microsoft Service for NetWare Directory Services to access resources on the NetWare 4.x server.

70-098.01.02.004

You are upgrading all Windows 95 workstations on a company's Windows NT domain to Windows 98. The PDC is using Windows NT Server 4.0 and has support for DFS resources. How can DFS resources be accessed from the Windows 98 workstations? (Choose two.)

▶ **Correct Answers: A and D**

    A. **Correct.** Windows 98 only supports SMB-based resources when using DFS.

    B. **Incorrect.** Windows 98 users cannot see non-SMB resources such as NetWare resources in a DFS tree.

    C. **Incorrect.** Windows 98 Client for Microsoft Networks supports DFS. No additional software needs to be installed.

    D. **Correct.** DFS provides a single path for accessing multiple shared resources on different servers across a network.

70-098.01.02.005

All network workstations use Windows 98 as their only operating system. The workstations need to access all of the network's resources. There are five Windows NT Server 4.0 servers, three NetWare 3.1 servers, and two NetWare 4.11 servers using NDS.

What must be installed on the network's workstations to access resources located on all servers? (Choose all that apply.)

▶ **Correct Answers: C and E**

    A. **Incorrect.** Although IPX/SPX is required, it is automatically installed when you configure the Microsoft Services for NetWare Directory Services.

    B. **Incorrect.** No additional protocols are required to access a Windows NT server's resources. Once you have installed Client for Microsoft Networks, your workstation will be able to participate on the network.

    C. **Correct.** Client for Microsoft Networks is required to access Windows NT server resources or other Microsoft-based operating system computers on a network. No additional protocols or network components are required for your computer to act as a network client.

    D. **Incorrect.** Since you are accessing NetWare NDS resources, you need to install the Microsoft Service for NetWare Directory Services, and therefore Client for NetWare Networks will be installed automatically. You do not need to install it separately.

    E. **Correct.** While Client for NetWare Networks will allow your workstation to appear as a Novell client to a NetWare server, you must install the Microsoft Service for NetWare Directory Services in order to access NDS resources.

70-098.01.02.006

Your network is configured as a workgroup with several Windows 98 and Windows NT Workstation 4.0 computers. Your company will soon implement a Windows NT domain to make the network more secure.

How will you access domain resources from the Windows 98 workstations?

A. Log on to the domain as a user who has the appropriate permissions to access the resource.

B. Log on to the workgroup as a user who has the appropriate permissions to access the resource.

C. Log on to the domain and access the resource as an authorized user using the Connect As option.

D. Log on to the workgroup and access the resource as an authorized user using the Connect As option.

70-098.01.02.007

You are designing a small network. The users would like to share files on their Windows 98 computers without having a dedicated server. Which security level would you recommend?

A. File-level security

B. User-level security

C. Share-level security

D. Directory-level security

70-098.01.02.006

Your network is configured as a workgroup with several Windows 98 and Windows NT Workstation 4.0 computers. Your company will soon implement a Windows NT domain to make the network more secure.

How will you access domain resources from the Windows 98 workstations?

▶ **Correct Answer: A**

A. **Correct.** Once a Windows NT domain has been implemented, users will log on to the domain to access network resources.

B. **Incorrect.** Users will no longer log on to their previous workgroup. Instead, users will log on to the Windows NT domain to access network resources.

C. **Incorrect.** Once users have been logged on to the domain, they will automatically be recognized by their user name. Use of the Connect As option is not required.

D. **Incorrect.** When using a Windows NT domain, users will automatically be recognized on the network by their user name. Use of the Connect As option is not required.

70-098.01.02.007

You are designing a small network. The users would like to share files on their Windows 98 computers without having a dedicated server. Which security level would you recommend?

▶ **Correct Answer: C**

A. **Incorrect.** Windows 98 does not support file-level security. Only Windows NT using the NTFS file system can provide this level of security.

B. **Incorrect.** Since there are no security providers to manage user accounts, user-level security cannot be used.

C. **Correct.** Since there is no dedicated server to act as a security provider, share-level security is the best solution.

D. **Incorrect.** Windows 98 does not support directory-level security. Consider using Windows NT and the NTFS file system to implement this level of security.

70-098.01.02.008

A small securities broker wants to know the ideal type of network for his office of five employees. He is very concerned about security. He wants the highest level of security possible.

Which solution fulfills his requirements?

A. Store the files on a security provider, and secure with share-level access control on the files.

B. Store the files on each user's Windows 98 computer using the FAT32 file system, and secure the computer with a security provider.

C. Store the files on a Windows NT Server 4.0 computer using the NTFS file system, and implement the appropriate access level for all users.

D. Store the files on each user's Windows 98 computer using the FAT file system, and secure the files with user-level access control at the file level.

E. Store the files on a Windows NT 4.0 computer using the FAT file system, and secure the files with user-level access control at the file level.

F. Store the files on a Windows NT Workstation 4.0 computer using the NTFS file system, and secure the files with user-level access control at the file level.

70-098.01.02.009

A network is composed of three Windows NT servers and 60 Windows 98 workstations. To tighten security, you need to disable the Modems, Passwords, and Users applets in Control Panel. Which Windows 98 tool can you use?

A. Task Manager

B. Registry Editor

C. System Policy Editor

D. System Information Utility

70-098.01.02.008

A small securities broker wants to know the ideal type of network for his office of five employees. He is very concerned about security. He wants the highest level of security possible.

Which solution fulfills his requirements?

▶ **Correct Answer: C**

A. **Incorrect.** Share-level access does not provide for the highest level of security since any user who knows the password will be able to access the files.

B. **Incorrect.** Although using a security provider to help implement user-level security is the best solution for Windows 98, the FAT32 file system does not provide for the highest level of security. Consider using NTFS and Windows NT for the highest level of security.

C. **Correct.** Only Windows NT support for NTFS provides for the highest level of security. In addition, NTFS supports auditing to track file and directory access.

D. **Incorrect.** Even with user-level security, the FAT file system does not provide secure access to its files.

E. **Incorrect.** Although Windows NT provides better security than Windows 98, using a FAT file system will not provide the highest level of security.

F. **Incorrect.** Although NTFS will provide the highest level of security, a Windows NT server should be used to provide better management of user access.

70-098.01.02.009

A network is composed of three Windows NT servers and 60 Windows 98 workstations. To tighten security, you need to disable the Modems, Passwords, and Users applets in Control Panel. Which Windows 98 tool can you use?

▶ **Correct Answer: C**

A. **Incorrect.** The Task Manager is not used to configure what applets are presented to the user.

B. **Incorrect.** The Registry Editor should only be used when other tools or utilities do not exist. In this case, a specific utility can be used to accomplish the desired results.

C. **Correct.** System policies will allow an administrator to control what applets are provided to the user based on his or her user name.

D. **Incorrect.** The System Information Utility is used to diagnose and solve system problems—not control what applets are presented to the user.

Further Reading

Microsoft Windows 98 Training Kit. Read Chapter 16, "Implementing Windows 98 System Policies," for an overview of system policies and how to create and manage them using System Policy Editor.

Microsoft Windows 98 Training Kit. Complete Lesson 1, "Identifying a User Profile," of Chapter 15, "Managing Windows 98 User Profiles." In this lesson, you will learn how Windows 98 implements user profiles.

Microsoft Windows 98 Training Kit. Complete Lesson 2, "Sharing Windows 98 Resources," of Chapter 12, "Configuring Windows 98 for Use on a Network." In this lesson, you will learn how Windows 98 can be configured to access a network. You will also learn how to install Client for Microsoft Networks and how to configure file and printer sharing.

Microsoft Windows 98 Training Kit. Complete Lesson 3, "Using Windows NT Network Resources," of Chapter 13, "Using Windows 98 on a Windows NT Network." In this lesson, you will learn how to use user-level security and assign permission to shared folders on a per-user basis.

Microsoft Windows 98 Resource Kit. Read Chapter 7, "User Profiles," for more details on how to effectively use user profiles to customize the user desktop.

Microsoft Windows 98 Resource Kit. Read Chapter 8, "System Policies," for more details on the benefits of system policies.

Windows 98 Accelerated MCSE Study Guide. Read Chapter 3, "Network Concepts," to learn more about how Windows 98 interacts with network resources.

Windows 98 Accelerated MCSE Study Guide. Read Chapter 9, "Network Security," to learn more about validating users in a network environment.

Installation and Configuration

This objective domain covers a number of topics; next to Troubleshooting, it is the largest domain. A good understanding of all the installation and configuration options for Windows 98 is important when preparing for the exam. Both local and network-based installations are covered. If you are used to installing Windows from a CD-ROM on a single computer, you will need to start thinking in terms of larger, enterprise-wide deployment. It is not reasonable, or efficient, to manually install Windows 98 on thousands of desktops. The use of a network install point and setup script can help automate this process.

How Windows 98 interacts with other operating systems in a dual boot environment is also covered. In addition, general networking support is also a major component of this objective domain. Not only is accessing a Microsoft network discussed, but so is connecting to a Novell NetWare network. You will need to become familiar with the features and requirements of NetWare when preparing for the exam. If you do not have access to a Novell network, be sure to carefully read the sources listed in the Further Reading sections at the end of each objective.

Windows 98 supports a variety of hardware and hardware-related features. Topics such as Universal Serial Bus (USB) and the OnNow power management technologies are covered. You'll need to know about these and how to configure them.

Tested Skills and Suggested Practices

The skills you need to successfully master the Installation and Configuration Objective Domain on the exam include:

- **Installing Windows 98.**

    - Practice 1: From a computer with no current operating system, install Windows 98 manually.

    - Practice 2: From a computer running Windows 95, upgrade the system to Windows 98.

- Practice 3: Install Windows 98 on a new system using a setup script to see how to automate the process. Consider customizing the script and running Setup again.

- Practice 4: Upgrade a system from Windows 95 to Windows 98. Once Windows 98 has been installed, uninstall it and return to the original operating system.

- **Installing Windows 98 server components.**

  - Practice 1: Install and configure the Microsoft Personal Web Server.

  - Practice 2: Using a Web browser, access files through the Personal Web Server (PWS).

  - Practice 3: Install Dial-Up Networking Server. Create a file share that can be accessed from other computers. Using a second computer and a modem, dial in to the first and access file resources.

- **Installing and configuring Client for Microsoft Networks.**

  - Practice 1: Install File and Printer Sharing for Microsoft Networks and share a local printer. Connect to the Windows 98 computer from another system on the network and test printing to the shared printer resource.

  - Practice 2: On a Windows 98 computer, share a folder. From a second computer on the local network, try to access files in the shared folder.

- **Configuring the Browse Master settings.**

  - Practice 1: Set up a workgroup of three or more Windows 98 computers each running File and Printer Sharing for Microsoft Networks. See which computer acts as the Browse Master by default.

  - Practice 2: Using the same workgroup from Practice 1, select a Windows 98 system that is not currently the Browse Master and configure it to always be the only Browse Master in the workgroup.

- **Configuring network protocols.**

  - Practice 1: Using a local area network with at least two Windows 98 computers, configure the systems to use NetBEUI. Use the Network Neighborhood to access each system.

  - Practice 2: Using the configuration from Practice 1, add the TCP/IP protocol and verify that the computers can access each other's resources.

- Practice 3: Remove the NetBEUI protocol from each of the computers in the previous Practice. Now test what level of network access is available. For example, the systems will no longer appear in Network Neighborhood. However, you can still ping each system and access HTML documents if one of them has the Microsoft Personal Web Server installed.

- **Using Microsoft Backup.**

  - Practice 1: Install and configure Microsoft Backup.

  - Practice 2: Use the Backup Wizard to back up, and then restore, sample files from the local computer.

  - Practice 3: Back up and restore the same files from Practice 2 without using the Backup Wizard.

Install Windows 98.

When installing Windows 98, you need to consider a number of installation options:

- Automated Windows setup

- New

- Upgrade

- Uninstall

- Dual boot combination with Microsoft Windows NT 4.0

Setup scripts are used to automate the Windows 98 Setup program. This text file allows you to predefine settings and is essential when installing Windows 98 on multiple computers. The setup script also allows you to install additional software. To use a setup script, run Setup on a computer and copy the appropriate sections from the SETUPLOG.TXT file. This file is created in the root directory of the C: drive. You can also edit an existing setup script file.

When you're installing Windows 98 on a computer as a new operating system, Setup will determine hardware settings automatically. This includes verifying that the computer meets the minimum hardware requirements. When you install Windows 98, Setup performs five phases:

- Phase 1—Preparing to run Windows 98 Setup

- Phase 2—Collecting information about your computer (this phase also creates the Emergency Startup Disk)

- Phase 3—Copying Windows 98 files to your computer

- Phase 4—Restarting your computer

- Phase 5—Setting up hardware and finalizing settings

These phases are essentially the same whether Setup is run from Windows 95, as an upgrade, or from an MS-DOS prompt.

Once Windows 98 is installed and configured properly, you can uninstall the previous version of Windows 95. Before removing Windows 95, you can use Add/Remove Programs to uninstall Windows 98. To do this, you must have saved the system files during setup. This will return the system to Windows 95.

While Windows 98 supports dual booting, it is not recommended to dual boot Windows 98 with Windows NT since Windows 98 does not support NTFS. In addition, Windows NT does not recognize FAT32.

To successfully answer the questions for this objective, you need a firm understanding of several key terms. For definitions of these terms, refer to the Glossary in this book.

Key Terms

- Dual boot

- FAT32

- Setup script

- Windows NT file system (NTFS)

70-098.02.01.001

Which Microsoft operating systems can dual boot with Windows 98? (Choose all that apply.)

A. Windows NT

B. Windows 95

C. Windows 3.x

D. MS-DOS 5.x or later

70-098.02.01.002

You want to dual boot Windows NT Workstation 4.0 and Windows 98 on your computer. What must you do so that both operating systems can use all applications on the computer?

A. Install Windows 98 on the C: drive.

B. Windows 98 must be installed on a FAT32 partition.

C. Windows NT must be installed first, then Windows 98.

D. Install each application twice, once under each operating system.

E. Uninstall Windows NT before setting up Windows 98, then install Windows 98.

F. Install Windows 98 first, then Windows NT; after the installation of Windows NT, convert the hard drive to NTFS.

70-098.02.01.001

Which Microsoft operating systems can dual boot with Windows 98? (Choose all that apply.)

▶ **Correct Answers: A, C, and D**

A. **Correct.** Windows 98 can dual boot to a Windows NT operating system, but this practice is not recommended since Windows 98 does not support the NTFS file system.

B. **Incorrect.** You cannot dual boot Windows 98 and Windows 95 because they both use the same boot files (IO.SYS, COMMAND.COM, and MSDOS.SYS).

C. **Correct.** Windows 98 can dual boot with Windows 3.x.

D. **Correct.** Windows 98 can dual boot with MS-DOS 5.x or later.

70-098.02.01.002

You want to dual boot Windows NT Workstation 4.0 and Windows 98 on your computer. What must you do so that both operating systems can use all applications on the computer?

▶ **Correct Answer: D**

A. **Incorrect.** Installing Windows 98 will not automatically allow all applications to run under both operating systems.

B. **Incorrect.** Windows NT does not support the FAT32 file system, so any application would not be accessible to Windows NT.

C. **Incorrect.** The order of OS installation will not affect whether all applications run under both systems.

D. **Correct.** Since each OS maintains its own system registry, applications will need to be installed twice to ensure they operate correctly under each OS.

E. **Incorrect.** Uninstalling Windows NT will not provide the ability to run all applications under both operating systems.

F. **Incorrect.** Since Windows 98 does not support NTFS, any application installed under Windows NT will be inaccessible to Windows 98.

70-098.02.01.003

Which of the following is required to install Windows 98?

A. CD-ROM

B. VGA video

C. 12 MB of RAM

D. Pentium processor

70-098.02.01.004

You are planning to upgrade a Windows 95 computer to Windows 98. What must be done before installing Windows 98? (Choose three.)

A. Disable all antivirus programs.

B. Disable any third-party memory managers.

C. Delete CONFIG.SYS before installing Windows 98.

D. Delete AUTOEXEC.BAT before installing Windows 98.

E. Load the real-mode CD-ROM drivers before starting setup.

F. Ensure that the computer meets the minimum requirements for the Windows 98 operating system.

70-098.02.01.003

Which of the following is required to install Windows 98?

▶ **Correct Answer: B**

   A. **Incorrect.** A CD-ROM is not required to install Windows 98. Windows 98 can be installed via a network, for example.

   B. **Correct.** Windows 98 does require a VGA video card.

   C. **Incorrect.** Windows 98 requires at least 16 MB of RAM.

   D. **Incorrect.** Windows 98 can be installed with a 486DX 66MHz processor.

70-098.02.01.004

You are planning to upgrade a Windows 95 computer to Windows 98. What must be done before installing Windows 98? (Choose three.)

▶ **Correct Answers: A, B, and F**

   A. **Correct.** Antivirus software can interfere with the Windows 98 Setup program and should be disabled before installing Windows 98.

   B. **Correct.** Memory managers can interfere with the Windows 98 Setup program and should be disabled before installing Windows 98.

   C. **Incorrect.** Assuming CONFIG.SYS does not load software that can interfere with the Windows 98 setup program, it does not have to be deleted.

   D. **Incorrect.** Assuming AUTOEXEC.BAT does not load software that can interfere with the Windows 98 Setup program, it does not have to be deleted.

   E. **Incorrect.** Windows 98 will automatically detect and install updated CD-ROM drivers, so real-mode drivers are not necessarily required.

   F. **Correct.** If the system does not meet the minimum requirements, Windows 98 will not install.

70-098.02.01.005

You are upgrading a Windows 3.1 computer to Windows 98. It is important to preserve your current settings. What is the best way to install Windows 98? (Choose two.)

A. Start Windows 98 Setup from MS-DOS.

B. Start Windows 98 Setup from within Windows 3.1.

C. Choose the existing Windows directory as the installation directory.

D. Type the command **<source file location>\setup/U** from the Windows 3.1 run line.

E. Choose another directory as the installation directory. Then use the Windows 3.1 upgrade utility.

70-098.02.01.006

You are concerned about upgrading your Windows 95 computer to Windows 98. You read on the Internet about a way to save and restore the existing Windows 95 configuration in case you want to remove Windows 98. What must you do to establish and preserve the option to revert to Windows 95? (Choose three.)

A. Convert the D: drive to FAT32.

B. Convert all partitions to FAT32.

C. Make sure that you do not delete the WINUNDO.DAT and WINUNDO.INI files.

D. Make sure you have an additional 50 MB of free disk space before setting up Windows 98.

E. Answer Yes in the Save System Files dialog box when prompted during Windows 98 Setup.

F. Make sure that you create an Emergency Startup Disk in case you want to remove Windows 98 and restore Windows 95.

70-098.02.01.005

You are upgrading a Windows 3.1 computer to Windows 98. It is important to preserve your current settings. What is the best way to install Windows 98? (Choose two.)

▶ **Correct Answers: A and C**

A. **Correct.** To upgrade from Windows 3.x, you must run the Windows 98 Setup program from MS-DOS. The current Windows 3.x configuration will then be preserved.

B. **Incorrect.** You cannot run the Windows 98 Setup program from within Windows 3.x.

C. **Correct.** You must tell the Windows 98 Setup program where the current version of Windows 3.x is installed. The current Windows settings will then be preserved.

D. **Incorrect.** You cannot run the Windows 98 Setup program from within Windows 3.x.

E. **Incorrect.** You must install Windows 98 to the same directory as Windows 3.x to preserve the configuration. In addition, there is no Windows 3.x upgrade utility for Windows 98.

70-098.02.01.006

You are concerned about upgrading your Windows 95 computer to Windows 98. You read on the Internet about a way to save and restore the existing Windows 95 configuration in case you want to remove Windows 98. What must you do to establish and preserve the option to revert to Windows 95? (Choose three.)

▶ **Correct Answers: C, D, and E**

A. **Incorrect.** No drives should be converted to FAT32 if they are to be restored to Windows 95.

B. **Incorrect.** All partitions should remain FAT16 if Windows 95 may be restored on this system.

C. **Correct.** Both the WINUNDO.DAT and WINUNDO.INI are required to return the system to Windows 95.

D. **Correct.** Windows 98 setup requires 50 MB of additional space to store Windows 95 system files.

E. **Correct.** Saving the Windows 95 system files is required if you want to return to the previous operating system.

F. **Incorrect.** The Emergency Startup Disk is used to recover from a Windows 98 failure. It is not used to restore the system to Windows 95.

70-098.02.01.007

A customer has a large Windows NT domain and needs to upgrade 400 Windows 95 computers to Windows 98. He wants to upgrade these computers in the most efficient way, while maintaining all of the existing desktop configurations. How would you recommend that this customer accomplish the upgrade? (Choose three.)

A. Create a setup script and store it on the Windows NT server.

B. Create a setup script and store it in the C:\Windows directory of all the workstations.

C. Change the values for the options to "1" to skip that option in the [Setup] section of the script.

D. Change the values for the options to "0" to choose no for all setup options in the [Setup] section of the script, which will allow for an unmanned installation of Windows 98.

E. Log on to the network and run Windows 98 Setup, specifying the path to the script file on the server.

F. Run Windows 98 Setup from CD-ROM, specifying the path to the script file on the workstations.

70-098.02.01.008

A network consists of a Windows NT server and 50 Windows 95 workstations. The network administrator seeks your advice about the fastest way to upgrade all of the workstations to Windows 98. He needs the upgrade to be performed by the user, but some of the workstations do not have CD-ROM drives. The network administrator does not want to incur any additional expenses.

How should this upgrade be performed?

A. Use Microsoft Systems Management Server (SMS) and implement a push installation in the evening hours.

B. Copy the Windows 98 source files to the Windows NT server so users can implement a push installation.

C. Copy the Windows 98 source files to the Windows NT server so users can implement a pull installation.

D. Add CD-ROM drives to the computers that currently do not have them, and have each user install from CD.

70-098.02.01.007

A customer has a large Windows NT domain and needs to upgrade 400 Windows 95 computers to Windows 98. He wants to upgrade these computers in the most efficient way, while maintaining all of the existing desktop configurations. How would you recommend that this customer accomplish the upgrade? (Choose three.)

▶ **Correct Answers: A, D, and E**

    A. **Correct.** Creating a setup script that can be accessed from a server will provide an automated setup process that will be consistent from computer to computer.

    B. **Incorrect.** To more efficiently use a setup script, it should be saved once in a shared network resource—not individually created on each client computer.

    C. **Incorrect.** Changing option values to 1 will not cause them to be skipped by the setup program.

    D. **Correct.** Changing option values to 0 will cause them to be skipped by the setup program, providing for a faster, more consistent setup.

    E. **Correct.** Using a network install and shared script file will ensure all the systems are configured the same way—in this case being sure to maintain existing user configurations.

    F. **Incorrect.** A network-based install point and setup script would be more efficient in this scenario.

70-098.02.01.008

A network consists of a Windows NT server and 50 Windows 95 workstations. The network administrator seeks your advice about the fastest way to upgrade all of the workstations to Windows 98. He needs the upgrade to be performed by the user, but some of the workstations do not have CD-ROM drives. The network administrator does not want to incur any additional expenses.

How should this upgrade be performed?

▶ **Correct Answer: C**

    A. **Incorrect.** Using SMS may incur additional costs and would not allow the users to install Windows 98 themselves.

    B. **Incorrect.** A push installation is designed to allow the administrator to control the installation on each user's computer. This is not the desired result in this scenario.

    C. **Correct.** Allowing for a pull installation would provide each user the ability to manage the Windows 98 setup individually.

    D. **Incorrect.** Since some of the computers do not have CD-ROMs, and the administrator does not want to incur additional costs, a network-based installation would be the correct solution.

Further Reading

Microsoft Windows 98 Training Kit. Complete Lesson 1, "Preparing for Installation," of Chapter 2, "Installing Windows 98." In this lesson, you will learn about minimum hardware requirements, dual booting Windows 98, and the various setup methods that you can choose from.

Microsoft Windows 98 Training Kit. Complete Lesson 2, "Upgrading from Windows 95," of Chapter 2, "Installing Windows 98." In this lesson, the five phases of setup are discussed and information about upgrading from Windows 95 is provided.

Microsoft Windows 98 Training Kit. Complete Lesson 4, "Automating Setup," of Chapter 2, "Installing Windows 98." In this lesson, you will learn about the use of setup scripts to help automate the installation of Windows 98 in a large environment.

Microsoft Windows 98 Training Kit. Complete Lesson 6, "Uninstalling Windows 98," of Chapter 2, "Installing Windows 98." In this lesson, the requirements to success-fully uninstall Windows 98 are discussed.

Windows 98 Accelerated MCSE Study Guide. Read Chapter 4, "Installing Windows 98," to learn more about the installation options provided by Windows 98.

OBJECTIVE 2.2

Configure Windows 98 Server Components.

Two main server components are presented on the exam:

■ Microsoft Personal Web Server 4.0

■ Dial-Up Networking Server

When the Microsoft Personal Web Server (PWS) component is installed on a Windows 98 computer, you can create, maintain, and test Web sites on the computer. The PWS has been designed for small networks in a peer-to-peer environment. The PWS will only allow 10 connections at one time. For a complete enterprise Web server, you will need to install Microsoft Internet Information Server on a Windows NT server. To use the PWS and Windows 98, the TCP/IP protocol must first be installed.

While the Microsoft Personal Web Server component allows access to Web pages, the Dial-Up Networking Server component allows for direct access to system resources. The Dial-Up Networking Server provides a single caller access to the system. Dial-Up Server is configured, along with security access, through Control Panel.

To successfully answer the questions for this objective, you need a firm understanding of several key terms. For definitions of these terms, refer to the Glossary in this book.

Key Terms

- Browse Master

- Data Link Control (DLC)

- Dial-Up Networking

- Dynamic Host Configuration Protocol (DHCP)

- File Transfer Protocol (FTP)

- Hypertext Transfer Protocol (HTTP)

- Internet

- Intranet

- Microsoft Personal Web Server (PWS)

- Peer-to-peer network

70-098.02.02.001

You want to use Personal Web Server on your Windows 98 computer to create a Web site for users on your intranet. What must be installed on your computer before you add Personal Web Server?

A. FTP

B. DHCP

C. Windows Internet Naming Service (WINS)

D. TCP/IP

E. IPX/SPX

70-098.02.02.002

Sally wants to use Personal Web Server (PWS) to publish a Web site for her intranet. Which Personal Web Server features should she be aware of that can affect the usage of her Web site? (Choose two.)

A. PWS requires DHCP.

B. PWS provides FTP service.

C. PWS only supports 10 user connections.

D. PWS allows a user to monitor traffic on her Web site.

70-098.02.02.003

Which protocols does Windows 98 Dial-Up Server support? (Choose all that apply.)

A. DLC

B. TCP/IP

C. IPX/SPX

D. NetBEUI

70-098.02.02.001

You want to use Personal Web Server on your Windows 98 computer to create a Web site for users on your intranet. What must be installed on your computer before you add Personal Web Server?

▶ **Correct Answer: D**

A. **Incorrect.** FTP is used to transfer files, not provide Web pages in a Web site.

B. **Incorrect.** While DHCP can be used to manage Internet Protocol (IP) addresses on an intranet, it is not required for Personal Web Server.

C. **Incorrect.** WINS is an optional solution for managing computer names on a Microsoft network. It is not required for Personal Web Server.

D. **Correct.** Personal Web Server requires the TCP/IP protocol to be installed on the computer.

E. **Incorrect.** IPX/SPX is not required to run PWS.

70-098.02.02.002

Sally wants to use Personal Web Server (PWS) to publish a Web site for her intranet. Which Personal Web Server features should she be aware of that can affect the usage of her Web site? (Choose two.)

▶ **Correct Answers: C and D**

A. **Incorrect.** Personal Web Server does not require DHCP.

B. **Incorrect.** Personal Web Server no longer supports the file transfer protocol. Consider Internet Information Server to support FTP services.

C. **Correct.** Personal Web Server is not designed for large Web sites and limits the number of concurrent users.

D. **Correct.** Personal Web Server does provide monitoring capabilities to track Web site usage.

70-098.02.02.003

Which protocols does Windows 98 Dial-Up Server support? (Choose all that apply.)

▶ **Correct Answers: C and D**

A. **Incorrect.** DLC (used for accessing special network resources such as an AS/400 or Hewlett-Packard network printer) does not work via a dial-up connection.

B. **Incorrect.** TCP/IP cannot be routed by Windows 98 and therefore is not supported by the Windows 98 Dial-Up Server.

C. **Correct.** IPX/SPX can be used over a dial-up connection to access NetWare resources.

D. **Correct.** NetBEUI can be used over a dial-up connection to access a Microsoft network.

70-098.02.02.004

Tom needs to access files on his work computer from his home. Both computers use Windows 98 as their only operating system. How must Tom's computers be configured to allow Tom access to his work computer from his home computer? (Choose three.)

A. Install a modem on the home computer.

B. Install user-level security on the work computer.

C. Install and configure Dial-Up Server on the work computer.

D. Use Dial-Up Networking on the home computer to access the work computer.

E. Ensure that Tom's work computer and his home computer have a protocol in common.

F. Install File and Printer Sharing on the work computer and enable share-level security.

70-098.02.02.004

Tom needs to access files on his work computer from his home. Both computers use Windows 98 as their only operating system. How must Tom's computers be configured to allow Tom access to his work computer from his home computer? (Choose three.)

▶ **Correct Answers: C, E, and F**

A. **Incorrect.** The question does not ask about the home computer, only the work computer, although a modem is required on the home system.

B. **Incorrect.** Since there is no server to manage accounts, share-level access should be implemented on the work computer.

C. **Correct.** Dial-Up Server is required for Tom to connect from home.

D. **Incorrect.** While Dial-Up Networking is required on the home computer, the question only asked about the work computer.

E. **Correct.** Both computers must have a common protocol.

F. **Correct.** File and Printer Sharing must be installed on the computer at work—however, file sharing may be the only option actually enabled.

70-098.02.02.005

A company has an eight-node, peer-to-peer Windows 98 network. The company only wants the computer named Server_01 to be the Browse Master. The computer's browser settings are as follows:

Server_01   Automatic

Client_01   Disabled

Client_02   Enabled

Client_03   Automatic

Client_04   Disabled

Client_05   Automatic

Client_06   Disabled

Client_07   Enabled

Which browser settings need to be changed so only Server_01 is the Browse Master? (Choose all that apply.)

A. Change Server_01 to enabled.

B. Change Client_03 and Client_05 to enabled.

C. Change Client_02 and Client_07 to automatic.

D. Change Client_01, Client_04, and Client_06 to enabled.

E. Change Client_01, Client_04, and Client_06 to automatic.

F. Change Client_02, Client_03, Client_05, and Client_07 to disabled.

70-098.02.02.005

A company has an eight-node, peer-to-peer Windows 98 network. The company only wants the computer named Server_01 to be the Browse Master. The computer's browser settings are as follows:

Server_01   Automatic

Client_01   Disabled

Client_02   Enabled

Client_03   Automatic

Client_04   Disabled

Client_05   Automatic

Client_06   Disabled

Client_07   Enabled

Which browser settings need to be changed so only Server_01 is the Browse Master? (Choose all that apply.)

▶ **Correct Answers: A and F**

A. **Correct.** The Browse Master must be set to enabled, not just automatic.

B. **Incorrect.** Only the Browse Master can be set to enabled.

C. **Incorrect.** To force a single computer to be the Browse Master, all other computers must be set to disabled.

D. **Incorrect.** Only the Browse Master can be set to enabled.

E. **Incorrect.** To force a single computer to be the Browse Master, it should be set to enabled, while all other computers should be set to disabled.

F. **Correct.** All other computers should be set to disabled.

70-098.02.02.006

A Windows 98 computer is primarily used to share files and applications. What must be done to optimize the computer for this role?

A. Open Control Panel, select the System icon, and set the File System properties from the General tab to network server.

B. Open Control Panel, select the System icon, and set the File System properties from the Performance tab to network server.

C. Open Control Panel, select the System icon, and set the File System properties from the Optimization tab to network server.

D. Open Control Panel, select the System icon, and set the File System properties from the Hardware Profiles tab to network server.

70-098.02.02.006

A Windows 98 computer is primarily used to share files and applications. What must be done to optimize the computer for this role?

▶ **Correct Answer: B**

A. **Incorrect.** You cannot set the File System properties to a network server from the General tab.

B. **Correct.** Under the system's Performance tab, the computer should be set to a network server.

C. **Incorrect.** You cannot set the File System properties to a network server from the Optimization tab.

D. **Incorrect.** You cannot set the File System properties from the Hardware Profile tab.

Further Reading

Microsoft Windows 98 Training Kit. Complete Lesson 3, "Sharing Resources on an Intranet," of Chapter 17, "Using Windows 98 and the Internet." In this lesson, you will learn about installing and configuring the Microsoft Personal Web Server component.

Microsoft Windows 98 Training Kit. Complete Lesson 2, "Configuring Dial-Up Networking Clients," of Chapter 18, "Implementing Dial-Up Networking in Windows 98." In this lesson, using both Dial-Up Networking client and server components will be discussed.

Windows 98 Accelerated MCSE Study Guide. Read Chapter 12, "Remote Connections," to learn more about the Dial-Up Networking and server capabilities of Windows 98.

OBJECTIVE 2.3

Install and configure the network components of Windows 98 in a Microsoft environment and a mixed Microsoft and NetWare environment.

Windows 98 includes a number of components that support both Microsoft and NetWare networks. However, before any network type can be accessed, a network adapter must be installed. Windows 98 Setup automatically detects most network cards and installs the appropriate driver. Once a network adapter has been configured, the appropriate network software can be installed. Network adapters, drivers, and software can be configured from the Network Neighborhood Properties window.

To access resources on a Microsoft network, you will need to install and configure Client for Microsoft Networks. An additional feature, File and Printer Sharing for Microsoft Networks, must also be installed before Windows 98 can share local files or printers. Similar components are provided for NetWare networks. Client for NetWare Networks and File and Printer Sharing for NetWare Networks must be installed in order for Windows 98 to access, or share, resources on a NetWare network.

Windows 98 clients can log on to Windows NT or NetWare servers. Before you can log on to a NetWare server, you have to install and configure the IPX/SPX protocol. If your network includes NetWare 4.x servers running NetWare Directory Services (NDS), you must install Service for NetWare Directory Services, which requires IPX/SPX-compatible Protocol and Client for NetWare Networks. If you do not install those components separately, Windows 98 installs them automatically with Service for NetWare Directory Services.

In addition to local area network support, Windows 98 can access private computers across the public Internet by using virtual private networking (VPN). VPN uses the Point-to-Point Tunneling Protocol (PPTP) to create a secure tunnel across an otherwise open network, such as the Internet. PPTP supports multiple protocols such as TCP/IP, IPX/SPX, and NetBEUI.

While Windows 98 can participate in a large Windows NT domain, you can also configure Windows 98 for use in a workgroup. In this case, the computers on the network will look for a Browse Master to provide information about the available systems currently on the network. Windows 98 will select the first computer that has File and Printer Sharing enabled to act as the Browse Master. A Windows 98 computer's browser property can be set to enabled, disabled, or automatic.

To successfully answer the questions for this objective, you need a firm understanding of several key terms. For definitions of these terms, refer to the Glossary in this book.

Key Terms

- Domain

- Interrupt request (IRQ)

- Network interface card (NIC)

- Network protocol

- Plug and Play

- Server Message Block (SMB)

- Workgroup

70-098.02.03.001

The network you are responsible for has one Windows NT domain and two workgroups. You would like to ensure that a specific Windows 98 computer will never become a Master Browser for its workgroup. How would you accomplish this?

A. Ensure that the Windows 98 computer logs on to the Windows NT domain.

B. Configure the Windows 98 computer to join the Windows NT domain.

C. Change the Browse Master setting in the Microsoft File and Print Services dialog on the computer to disabled.

D. Change the Browse Master setting in the Microsoft File and Print Services dialog on another Windows 98 computer to enabled.

70-098.02.03.002

Which networking protocols does Client for Microsoft Networks support? (Choose all that apply.)

A. IPX

B. DLC

C. TCP/IP

D. NetBEUI

70-098.02.03.001

The network you are responsible for has one Windows NT domain and two workgroups. You would like to ensure that a specific Windows 98 computer will never become a Master Browser for its workgroup. How would you accomplish this?

▶ **Correct Answer: C**

A. **Incorrect.** Changing from a workgroup logon to a domain logon is not the most efficient solution.

B. **Incorrect.** Changing from a workgroup logon to a domain logon is not the most efficient solution.

C. **Correct.** Changing the Browse Master setting to disabled is the only way to ensure that this computer will not act as a Browse Master in a workgroup.

D. **Incorrect.** Changing the Browse Master setting to enabled will force this computer to always act as a Browse Master.

70-098.02.03.002

Which networking protocols does Client for Microsoft Networks support? (Choose all that apply.)

▶ **Correct Answers: A, C, and D**

A. **Correct.** Client for Microsoft Networks has built-in support for the IPX protocol.

B. **Incorrect.** Client for Microsoft Networks does not support the DLC protocol. You must install Microsoft 32-bit DLC to access DLC network resources.

C. **Correct.** Client for Microsoft Networks has built-in support for the TCP/IP protocol.

D. **Correct.** Client for Microsoft Networks has built-in support for the NetBEUI protocol.

70-098.02.03.003

Which networking components need to be installed on a Windows 98 computer in order to access files and printers on a Windows NT server? (Choose four.)

A. The SMB protocol

B. Client for Microsoft Networks

C. File and Printer Sharing for Microsoft Networks

D. A Windows 98–compatible network adapter or modem

E. Appropriate networking cable to attach to the local area network

F. The same networking protocol that the Windows NT server is using

70-098.02.03.004

A client needs to upgrade all workstations from Windows for Workgroups 3.11 to Windows 98. The client would like to use all existing network adapter cards and cabling. The computer's hardware is not Plug and Play–compatible and is at least three years old. How should these network adapter cards be configured?

A. Windows 98 will only work with Plug and Play network adapter cards.

B. Windows 98 will require you to manually add the driver from the manufacturer's driver installation disk.

C. Windows 98 will require you to manually reset the IRQ settings on the network adapter card to match the Network options in Control Panel.

D. Windows 98 will start the Add New Hardware Wizard and attempt to automatically configure itself to match the current settings of the network adapter card.

70-098.02.03.003

Which networking components need to be installed on a Windows 98 computer in order to access files and printers on a Windows NT server? (Choose four.)

▶ **Correct Answers: B, D, E, and F**

    A. **Incorrect.** SMB is not required to access files on a Windows NT server.

    B. **Correct.** Client for Microsoft Networks is required before the Windows 98 client can "see" a Windows NT network.

    C. **Incorrect.** File and Printer Sharing is required only if this Windows 98 computer will share its resources.

    D. **Correct.** A NIC and appropriate driver are required to access the network.

    E. **Correct.** The appropriate network cable is required to physically connect the computer to the network.

    F. **Correct.** Both computers must be configured with the same protocol before the Windows 98 computer can access Windows NT shared resources.

70-098.02.03.004

A client needs to upgrade all workstations from Windows for Workgroups 3.11 to Windows 98. The client would like to use all existing network adapter cards and cabling. The computer's hardware is not Plug and Play–compatible and is at least three years old. How should these network adapter cards be configured?

▶ **Correct Answer: D**

    A. **Incorrect.** Windows 98 will work with legacy hardware that is not Plug and Play–compliant.

    B. **Incorrect.** Windows 98 can automatically configure itself to work with hardware that is not Plug and Play–compliant, using the Add New Hardware Wizard.

    C. **Incorrect.** Windows 98 will attempt to use existing IRQ settings for configured hardware.

    D. **Correct.** Since the NIC has already been configured successfully in this system, Windows 98 should be able to use those settings automatically.

70-098.02.03.005

You install a legacy network adapter card in a Windows 98 computer and boot it. The Add New Hardware detection process begins and recommends using IRQ 7 for the network card. You know the jumper settings on the card are set for IRQ 5.

What should you do to resolve this problem?

A. Use Device Manager to check for conflicting devices at IRQ 5.

B. Reject the proposed setting and set the IRQ to 5 to match the card.

C. Accept the proposed setting. Windows 98 will remap all IRQ requests.

D. Change the jumper setting on the card to IRQ 7 and run Add New Hardware again.

70-098.02.03.006

You are using Windows 98 computers to access several NetWare servers on a network. A NetWare server must validate the users of the workstations. How can you configure Client for NetWare networks to automatically log on to a NetWare server for authentication?

A. Set the preferred server name in the IPX/SPX Properties General tab.

B. Add "PREFERRED SERVER = SERVERX" to the NET.SYS file of each workstation.

C. Add "PREFERRED SERVER = SERVERX" to the CONFIG.SYS file of each workstation.

D. Choose a preferred server name in the Client for NetWare Networks Properties General tab.

70-098.02.03.005

You install a legacy network adapter card in a Windows 98 computer and boot it. The Add New Hardware detection process begins and recommends using IRQ 7 for the network card. You know the jumper settings on the card are set for IRQ 5.

What should you do to resolve this problem?

▶ **Correct Answer: D**

A. **Incorrect.** Checking for conflicting IRQs will not resolve this issue.

B. **Incorrect.** Windows 98 will automatically configure the IRQs that it can—forcing Windows 98 to use IRQ 5 may cause a conflict with another device.

C. **Incorrect.** Windows 98 cannot change the physical setting on a card. You will need to manually change the setting on the NIC to IRQ 7 and then rerun the Add New Hardware Wizard.

D. **Correct.** Only if you manually change the IRQ to 7 and then rerun Add New Hardware Wizard will Windows 98 be able to configure the system correctly.

70-098.02.03.006

You are using Windows 98 computers to access several NetWare servers on a network. A NetWare server must validate the users of the workstations. How can you configure Client for NetWare Networks to automatically log on to a NetWare server for authentication?

▶ **Correct Answer: D**

A. **Incorrect.** The IPX/SPX protocol entry does not have a General tab.

B. **Incorrect.** When using Client for NetWare Networks, you do not need to use the NET.SYS file to configure a preferred server.

C. **Incorrect.** When using Client for NetWare Networks, you do not need to use the CONFIG.SYS file to configure a preferred server.

D. **Correct.** Using Client for NetWare Networks, you can configure a preferred NetWare server.

70-098.02.03.007

You just completed upgrading several Windows 95 workstations on a NetWare 4.x network to Windows 98. You expected Windows 98 to automatically install Client for NetWare Networks because your MS-DOS clients are running NetWare 3.x client software (NETX). After Setup completes, you discover that the Client for NetWare Networks is not installed.

Which conditions could have prevented Windows 98 from installing Client for NetWare Networks? (Choose three.)

A. The IPX/SPX protocol must be installed first.

B. The Windows 95 client was configured to run LOGIN.EXE from a batch file.

C. The Windows 95 client was configured to run only with real-mode client software.

D. Some terminate-and-stay resident programs (TSRs) are present that are not compatible with Client for NetWare Networks.

E. Some TSRs are present that are not compatible with other protected-mode components.

F. The File and Printer Sharing for NetWare Networks service must be installed before installing Client for NetWare Networks.

0-098.02.03.007

You just completed upgrading several Windows 95 workstations on a NetWare 4.x network to Windows 98. You expected Windows 98 to automatically install Client for NetWare Networks because your MS-DOS clients are running NetWare 3.x client software (NETX). After Setup completes, you discover that Client for NetWare Networks is not installed.

Which conditions could have prevented Windows 98 from installing Client for NetWare Networks? (Choose three.)

▶ **Correct Answers: B, D, and E**

A. **Incorrect.** When you install Client for NetWare Networks, the IPX/SPX protocol will be installed automatically—it is not required beforehand.

B. **Correct.** Windows 98 Setup will automatically remove any reference to LOGIN.EXE. However, in this case, Setup will not automatically install Client for NetWare Networks component.

C. **Incorrect.** Windows 98 and Client for NetWare Networks do not require real-mode client software.

D. **Correct.** You should first manually remove any TSRs since Windows 98 Setup will not automatically remove them.

E. **Correct.** You should first manually remove any TSRs since Windows 98 Setup will not automatically remove them.

F. **Incorrect.** File and Printer Sharing for NetWare Networks is not required to have Windows 98 automatically install Client for NetWare Networks.

70-098.02.03.008

Which capabilities are provided if the Windows 98 version of Client for NetWare Networks and Microsoft Service for NetWare Directory Services are installed? (Choose all that apply.)

A. You can use any utility that requires NDS.

B. The RPRINTER utility can be used with NetWare 3.x.

C. You can run most bindery-based NetWare 4.x utilities.

D. Capture commands in the logon scripts can use the NDS format.

E. You can run all NetWare 3.x utilities that reside on the NetWare server, such as SYSCON.

F. You can use the 32-bit, protected-mode graphical tools built into Windows 98, as well as the 16-bit command-line utilities provided with NetWare for managing and sharing resources.

70-098.02.03.009

A Windows 98 workstation is connected to a Novell NetWare 4.x network. Which Windows 98 networking component must be installed to access resources using NetWare Directory Services?

A. IPX/SPX

B. Microsoft Client for NetWare Networks

C. Microsoft Service for NetWare Directory Services

D. Microsoft File and Printer Sharing for NetWare Networks

770-098.02.03.008

Which capabilities are provided if the Windows 98 version of Client for NetWare Networks and Microsoft Service for NetWare Directory Services are installed? (Choose all that apply.)

▶ **Correct Answers: A, C, E, and F**

A. **Correct.** Once Microsoft Service for NetWare Directory Services is installed, Windows 98 provides NDS capabilities.

B. **Incorrect.** RPRINTER is not required when using Microsoft Client for NetWare Networks with Windows 98.

C. **Correct.** When connecting to a Novell server using Microsoft Client for NetWare Networks, you can use most bindery-based utilities.

D. **Incorrect.** You cannot capture commands in logon scripts when using Microsoft Client for NetWare Networks or Microsoft Service for NetWare Directory Services.

E. **Correct.** Once Microsoft Client for NetWare Networks is installed, you can run all utilities that reside on a Novell server, such as SYSCON. Utilities that require NDS cannot be used until Microsoft Service for NetWare Directory Services is installed as well.

F. **Correct.** With both Client for NetWare Networks and Microsoft Service for NetWare Directory Services installed, almost all of the Novell functionality you require will be made available.

70-098.02.03.009

A Windows 98 workstation is connected to a Novell NetWare 4.x network. Which Windows 98 networking component must be installed to access resources using NetWare Directory Services?

▶ **Correct Answer: C**

A. **Incorrect.** Although IPX/SPX is required to access a NetWare server, it alone does not support NetWare Directory Services.

B. **Incorrect.** While Client for NetWare Networks offers additional services supported by NetWare servers, you need to install additional software to access NetWare Directory Services.

C. **Correct.** Microsoft Service for NetWare Directory Services must be installed before a Windows 98 client supports NDS.

D. **Incorrect.** Microsoft File and Printer Sharing for NetWare Networks does not provide Windows 98 users access to NDS.

70-098.02.03.010

Your Windows 98 computer is connected to a NetWare network. How can you access file resources on the NetWare server?

A. You must map a drive to the NetWare server where the file resource is located.

B. You must connect to the NetWare drive before you can access any file resources.

C. You must map a drive to the volume on the NetWare server where the file resource is located.

D. You can use the Network Neighborhood to view and attach to a NetWare server where the file resource is located.

70-098.02.03.011

You need to share a Windows 98 computer's My Documents folder with six NetWare 3.11 client computers. Which components must be installed on the Windows 98 computer to allow the NetWare clients network access to the folder? (Choose all that apply.)

A. NETX

B. TCP/IP

C. Client for NetWare Networks

D. An IPX/SPX-compatible protocol

E. Service for NetWare Directory Services

F. File and Printer Sharing for NetWare Networks

70-098.02.03.010

Your Windows 98 computer is connected to a NetWare network. How can you access file resources on the NetWare server?

► **Correct Answer: D**

A. **Incorrect**. To access a NetWare server resource, you do not necessarily have to map a drive first. You can browse to the resource using Network Neighborhood and access the files directly.

B. **Incorrect.** Connecting to the NetWare drive is not necessarily required to access files on the resource. You can browse to the resource using Network Neighborhood and access the files directly.

C. **Incorrect.** To access a NetWare server resource, you do not necessarily have to map a drive first. You can browse to the resource using Network Neighborhood and access the files directly.

D. **Correct.** Using Windows 98 Network Neighborhood, you can browse to the server and the appropriate resource to access the necessary files.

70-098.02.03.011

You need to share a Windows 98 computer's My Documents folder with six NetWare 3.11 client computers. Which components must be installed on the Windows 98 computer to allow the NetWare clients network access to the folder? (Choose all that apply.)

► **Correct Answers: C, D, and F**

A. **Incorrect.** NETX is not required when Client for NetWare Networks is installed.

B. **Incorrect.** NetWare networks use the IPX/SPX protocol.

C. **Correct.** Client for NetWare Networks will allow the Windows 98 computer access to a NetWare network.

D. **Correct.** NetWare networks use the IPX/SPX-compatible protocol.

E. **Incorrect.** NDS is not required on the Windows 98 computer to share its resources to other NetWare clients.

F. **Correct.** File and Printer Sharing for NetWare Networks is required before Windows 98 can share its resources to NetWare clients.

70-098.02.03.012

A Windows 98 computer is part of a Windows NT domain. A user needs to share her Accounting folder with seven other members of the accounting department. She does not want the folder placed on a Windows NT server.

Which networking component can you add to her Windows 98 computer to allow her to share the file?

A. Client for Microsoft Networks

B. Gateway Services for Microsoft Networks

C. Workgroup Services for Microsoft Networks

D. File and Printer Sharing for Microsoft Networks

70-098.02.03.013

Your Windows 98 computer is connected to a Windows NT domain. You want to allow certain domain users access to a folder on your computer. Which components should be added to your computer to enable you to share the file from your computer and still provide a high level of security? (Choose two.)

A. Install Peer Resource Sharing for Microsoft Networks.

B. Install File and Printer Sharing for Microsoft Networks.

C. Implement user-level security through Control Panel's Network utility.

D. Implement share-level security through Control Panel's Network utility.

E. Implement user-level security on the Windows 98 computer, and set up the Windows NT domain for workgroup security.

70-098.02.03.012

A Windows 98 computer is part of a Windows NT domain. A user needs to share her Accounting folder with seven other members of the accounting department. She does not want the folder placed on a Windows NT server.

Which networking component can you add to her Windows 98 computer to allow her to share the file?

▶ **Correct Answer: D**

   A. **Incorrect.** Client for Microsoft Networks alone will not allow a Windows 98 user to share their resources.

   B. **Incorrect.** Gateway Services for Microsoft Networks is not supported by Windows 98.

   C. **Incorrect.** Workgroup Services for Microsoft Networks is not supported by Windows 98.

   D. **Correct.** You must first install File and Printer Services for Microsoft Networks (and then turn on File Sharing) before other clients can access a Windows 98 folder.

70-098.02.03.013

Your Windows 98 computer is connected to a Windows NT domain. You want to allow certain domain users access to a folder on your computer. Which components should be added to your computer to enable you to share the file from your computer and still provide a high level of security? (Choose two.)

▶ **Correct Answers: B and C**

   A. **Incorrect.** Peer Resource Sharing for Microsoft Networks is not supported by Windows 98.

   B. **Correct.** File and Printer Sharing for Microsoft Networks is required before Windows 98 will share files (or folders).

   C. **Correct.** Since there is a Windows NT domain, you can implement user-level security to provide the highest level of security.

   D. **Incorrect.** Share-level security does not provide higher security than user-level.

   E. **Incorrect.** A Windows NT domain provides the highest level of user-based security on a network.

Further Reading

Microsoft Windows 98 Training Kit. Complete Lesson 1, "Installing and Configuring Network Components," of Chapter 12, "Configuring Windows 98 for Use on a Network." In this lesson, you will learn how to configure Windows 98 to support a network.

Microsoft Windows 98 Resource Kit. Read pages 660–671 to learn more about configuring and supporting network adapters.

Microsoft Windows 98 Training Kit. Complete Lesson 2, "Sharing Windows 98 Resources," of Chapter 12, "Configuring Windows 98 for Use on a Network." In this lesson, installing and configuring Client for Microsoft Networks and File and Printer Sharing are discussed. How to configure a Browse Master is also demonstrated.

Microsoft Windows 98 Training Kit. Complete Lesson 2, "Logging on to a NetWare Server," of Chapter 14, "Using Windows 98 on a Novell Network." In this lesson, configuring IPX/SPX and the NetWare network components is discussed.

Microsoft Windows 98 Training Kit. Complete Lesson 4, "Sharing Resources with NetWare Users," of Chapter 14, "Using Windows 98 on a Novell Network." In this lesson, you will learn how to install and configure Client for NetWare Networks and File and Printer Sharing.

Microsoft Windows 98 Training Kit. Complete Lesson 2, "Configuring Dial-Up Networking Clients," of Chapter 18, "Implementing Dial-Up Networking in Windows 98." In this lesson, using virtual private networking and other dial-up features is discussed.

Microsoft Windows 98 Resource Kit. Read pages 885–893 to learn more about configuring and supporting virtual private networking.

Windows 98 Accelerated MCSE Study Guide. Read Chapter 8, "Network Configuration," to learn more about how Windows 98 supports network connectivity.

OBJECTIVE 2.4

Install and configure network protocols in a Microsoft environment and a mixed Microsoft and NetWare environment.

Windows 98 supports a number of network protocols including:

- NetBEUI

- IPX/SPX

- TCP/IP

- Microsoft DLC

- Fast Infrared

Once a network device has been installed, you must configure the appropriate network protocol before Windows 98 can interact with another computer across a network. Both computers must run the same protocol in order for communication to take place. To install and configure network protocols, use the Network Neighborhood Properties page.

Depending on the type of network Windows 98 will connect to, a specific protocol must be selected. For example, local area networks that are running Microsoft operating systems should use the NetBEUI protocol. However, NetBEUI does not route and cannot be used in a wide area network environment, or over the Internet. If your organization requires access to remote networks, you will need to select an alternative routable protocol, such as TCP/IP. Likewise, if the Windows 98 computer will be connecting to a Novell NetWare network, the IPX/SPX protocol should be used. The Microsoft DLC protocol must be used if there are any Hewlett-Packard network printers or IBM AS/400 resources that will be accessed. Overall, the choice of protocol is critical to ensure that Windows 98 has efficient access to the network resources that are available.

To successfully answer the questions for this objective, you need a firm understanding of several key terms. For definitions of these terms, refer to the Glossary in this book.

Key Terms

- Data Link Control (DLC)

- Dynamic Host Configuration Protocol (DHCP)

- IPX/SPX

- NetBIOS Extended User Interface (NetBEUI)

- Network printer

- Network protocol

- Point-to-Point Protocol (PPP)

- Routing

- Serial Line Interface Protocol (SLIP)

- TCP/IP

70-098.02.04.001

Examine the Windows IP configuration shown below.

This Windows 98 computer cannot access a server on another segment of a Windows NT domain.

What is the problem?

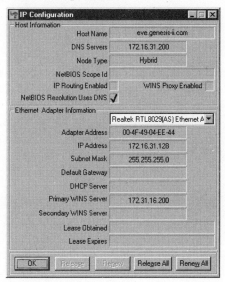

A. No IP routing is enabled.

B. No DHCP address is configured.

C. No Default Gateway is configured.

D. No Secondary WINS server is configured.

70-098.02.04.001

Examine the Windows IP configuration shown on the previous page.

This Windows 98 computer cannot access a server on another segment of a Windows NT domain.

What is the problem?

▶ **Correct Answer: C**

A. **Incorrect.** You cannot configure IP routing in Windows 98.

B. **Incorrect.** A DHCP server provides IP information, but is not required to access other segments of the network.

C. **Correct.** A Default Gateway must be configured before a host can access another network segment.

D. **Incorrect.** WINS provides computer name information. It does not support accessing other network segments.

70-098.02.04.002

Which networking protocols does Windows 98 support? (Choose all that apply.)

A. Network Device Interface Specification (NDIS)

B. TCP/IP

C. NetBEUI

D. IPX/SPX

E. 32-bit DLC

70-098.02.04.003

A corporation's headquarters has a Windows NT domain with 150 Windows 98 computers, 40 Windows NT Workstation 4.0 computers, and 7 Windows NT Server 4.0 computers. The corporation also has 15 remote sites, which each have 10 computers. The remote sites are connected to the corporate headquarters via routers and T1 connections.

Which single protocol is best for the entire network?

A. TCP/IP

B. NetBEUI

C. IPX/SPX

D. DLC and NetBEUI

E. TCP/IP and NetBEUI

70-098.02.04.002

Which networking protocols does Windows 98 support? (Choose all that apply.)

▶ **Correct Answers: B, C, D, and E**

A. **Incorrect.** NDIS is not a network protocol.

B. **Correct.** Windows 98 supports a number of network protocols, including TCP/IP.

C. **Correct.** Windows 98 supports a number of network protocols, including NetBEUI.

D. **Correct.** Windows 98 supports a number of network protocols, including IPX/SPX.

E. **Correct.** Windows 98 supports a number of network protocols, including DLC.

70-098.02.04.003

A corporation's headquarters has a Windows NT domain with 150 Windows 98 computers, 40 Windows NT Workstation 4.0 computers, and 7 Windows NT Server 4.0 computers. The corporation also has 15 remote sites, which each have 10 computers. The remote sites are connected to the corporate headquarters via routers and T1 connections.

Which single protocol is best for the entire network?

▶ **Correct Answer: A**

A. **Correct.** TCP/IP provides the best routable protocol for use over a wide area network (WAN).

B. **Incorrect.** NetBEUI works best on a local area network (LAN) but is not the best solution for a wide area network (WAN).

C. **Incorrect.** IPX/SPX works well on a NetWare network, but since this environment is both a Microsoft network and a WAN, IPX/SPX would not be the best choice.

D. **Incorrect.** DLC and NetBEUI are not the best solution for a WAN.

E. **Incorrect.** TCP/IP and NetBEUI would not be the most efficient protocol solution in this example due to the WAN requirements.

70-098.02.04.004

You are connecting 15 new Windows 98 computers to the corporate IBM AS/400 network. Which networking protocol must be installed on the Windows 98 computers to allow the computers to use host terminal emulation software to connect to the AS/400 server?

A. DLC

B. TCP/IP

C. IPX/SPX

D. NetBEUI

70-098.02.04.005

You are dialing in to a Windows 98 computer using Dial-Up Server. Which computers and protocols can be used to dial in to the Windows 98 computers? (Choose all that apply.)

A. Windows NT using PPP

B. Windows NT using SLIP

C. Windows 95 using SLIP

D. Windows for Workgroups using PPP

E. Windows 95 using Asynchronous NetBEUI

F. Windows for Workgroups using Asynchronous NetBEUI

70-098.02.04.004

You are connecting 15 new Windows 98 computers to the corporate IBM AS/400 network. Which networking protocol must be installed on the Windows 98 computers to allow the computers to use host terminal emulation software to connect to the AS/400 server?

▶ **Correct Answer: A**

A. **Correct.** Microsoft DLC (Data Link Control) is a protocol specifically designed to be used with network resources such as AS/400s and Hewlett-Packard network printers.

B. **Incorrect.** TCP/IP is not designed to be used to access an AS/400.

C. **Incorrect.** IPX/SPX is not designed to be used to access an AS/400.

D. **Incorrect.** NetBEUI is not designed to be used to access an AS/400.

70-098.02.04.005

You are dialing in to a Windows 98 computer using Dial-Up Server. Which computers and protocols can be used to dial in to the Windows 98 computers? (Choose all that apply.)

▶ **Correct Answers: A, D, E, and F**

A. **Correct.** Windows 98 as a dial-up server supports Point-to-Point Protocol (PPP).

B. **Incorrect.** Windows 98 as a dial-up server does not currently support Serial Line Internet Protocol (SLIP).

C. **Incorrect.** Windows 98 as a dial-up server does not currently support SLIP.

D. **Correct.** Windows 98 as a dial-up server supports PPP.

E. **Correct.** Windows 98 as a dial-up server supports the NetBEUI protocol.

F. **Correct.** Windows 98 as a dial-up server supports the NetBEUI protocol.

Further Reading

Microsoft Windows 98 Training Kit. Complete Lesson 1, "Installing and Configuring Network Components," of Chapter 12, "Configuring Windows 98 for Use on a Network." In this lesson, you will learn how to configure Windows 98 to support a network.

Microsoft Windows 98 Resource Kit. Read page 1350 to learn more about the architectural relationship between network adapters, drivers, and protocols in Windows 98.

Microsoft Windows 98 Training Kit. Complete Lesson 2, "Logging on to a NetWare Server," of Chapter 14, "Using Windows 98 on a Novell Network." In this lesson, you will learn how to configure Windows 98 to access a NetWare network.

Microsoft Windows 98 Resource Kit. Read pages 856–857 to learn more about the different local area network protocols.

Microsoft Windows 98 Training Kit. Complete Lesson 2, "Configuring Dial-Up Networking Clients," of Chapter 18, "Implementing Dial-Up Networking in Windows 98." In this lesson, using virtual private networking and other dial-up features will be discussed.

Windows 98 Accelerated MCSE Study Guide. Read Chapter 8, "Network Configuration," to learn more about the various network protocols supported by Windows 98.

Install and configure hardware devices in a Microsoft environment and a mixed Microsoft and NetWare environment.

In addition to various network protocol and network operating system support, Windows 98 supports a variety of hardware devices. These include the following:

- Modems

- Printers

- Universal Serial Bus (USB)

- Multiple Display Support

- IEEE 1394 FireWire

- Infrared Data Association (IrDA)

- Multilink

- Power management scheme

When using a modem or Integrated Services Digital Network (ISDN) device, Windows 98 can access remote networks through Dial-Up Networking. Dial-Up Networking can be used to establish connections to a remote server. This feature is useful for employees who require remote access to the network and for those who require Internet access on demand in a company not connected to the Internet. If a modem is being used to set up Dial-Up Networking, it must be installed and configured using Control Panel. You must then configure the dial-up adapter. To have access to ISDN service, you must install an ISDN adapter and run the ISDN Configuration Wizard, which prompts you for the Switch protocol, telephone numbers, and service profile identification (SPID) numbers. ISDN drivers from the ISDN 1.0 Accelerator Pack are not supported in Windows 98.

Windows 98 supports a variety of printers. To install a printing device, Windows 98 can automatically detect local printers via Plug and Play detection, or you can run the Add Printer Wizard.

Support for Universal Serial Bus (USB) is also included. USB provides access to a variety of peripherals such as mouse devices, keyboards, joysticks, scanners, audio devices, and digital cameras. When using USB-compliant peripherals, up to 127 such devices can be attached simultaneously. Since USB is Plug and Play–compatible, you can "hot swap" USB peripherals without having to reboot. USB also supports an external bus, so devices can be attached and removed without opening the computer case.

New to the Windows operating system is support for multiple displays. This means you can have more than one monitor attached to a single computer. In addition, Multiple Display Support allows for more than one graphic adapter to be installed in the computer. Up to nine monitors can be used on a single system.

Windows 98 supports the IEEE 1394 bus, also known as FireWire. It is designed for high-bandwidth PC devices, such as digital camcorders, cameras, and videodisc players. IEEE 1394 is similar to USB, except that it supports devices requiring much higher bandwidth. IEEE 1394 devices are Plug and Play–compatible, so when installing an IEEE 1394 device, you do not have to restart the computer to enable the new device. Since IEEE 1394 is an external bus, you can add a device without having to open the computer.

The default Dial-Up Networking settings are appropriate for most dial-up connections. However, you can also use multiple physical links (Multilink) with a single connection to increase transmission bandwidth and speed. Windows 98 supports the Multilink Point-to-Point Protocol (MPPP) to increase data transmission rates. Multilink can be configured through the Dial-Up Networking connection properties.

Windows 98 also supports the OnNow power management scheme. Under this scheme, a computer can appear to be turned off but is actually on and able to respond immediately to user requests. System requirements for OnNow include Advanced Configuration and Power Interface (ACPI). Peripherals must meet ACPI specifications, and applications must support power management and be Plug and Play–compatible. To configure OnNow, use the Power Management icon in the Control Panel.

To successfully answer the questions for this objective, you need a firm understanding of several key terms. For definitions of these terms, refer to the Glossary in this book.

Key Terms

- Extended Capabilities Port (ECP)

- Hot swap

- Multiple Display Support

- Plug and Play

- Universal Serial Bus (USB)

70-098.02.05.001

What are three features of Universal Serial Bus (USB)? (Choose three.)

A. USB can support up to 147 devices.

B. USB devices must be Plug and Play–compatible.

C. USB requires special drivers for external hardware devices.

D. USB requires only one computer restart when a new USB device is added.

E. USB hardware devices can be connected externally to the Windows 98 computer.

F. USB eliminates the need to install additional dedicated adapter cards inside the computer for new hardware devices.

70-098.02.05.002

How does Windows 98 support USB devices? (Choose two.)

A. Windows 98 supports only bus-powered devices.

B. Windows 98 does not support the "suspend power" mode.

C. Windows 98 does not support hot plug-in play for USB devices.

D. USB allows you to attach up to 127 devices to the bus simultaneously.

E. Windows 98 uses detection and enumeration to identify a newly connected device.

70-098.02.05.001

What are three features of Universal Serial Bus (USB)? (Choose three.)

▶ **Correct Answers: B, E, and F**

A. **Incorrect.** USB supports up to 127 devices, not 147.

B. **Correct.** All USB devices must conform to the Plug and Play standard.

C. **Incorrect.** USB will automatically configure the appropriate driver for the device.

D. **Incorrect.** USB allows for "hot swapping" of devices. You can install and remove devices without rebooting Windows 98.

E. **Correct.** USB devices can be daisy-chained to allow for multiple external devices.

F. **Correct.** Through the USB port, devices can easily be plugged directly into the computer or daisy-chained off one another.

70-098.02.05.002

How does Windows 98 support USB devices? (Choose two.)

▶ **Correct Answers: D and E**

A. **Incorrect.** Windows 98 supports bus-powered and externally powered devices.

B. **Incorrect.** Windows 98 supports three power modes: on, suspend, and off.

C. **Incorrect.** Windows 98 allows for hot swapping of USB devices.

D. **Correct.** You can attach up to 127 devices simultaneously.

E. **Correct.** Windows 98 allows you to plug a USB device into the computer and will configure it automatically.

70-098.02.05.003

What are the three types of USB components? (Choose three.)

A. Hub

B. Unit

C. Port

D. Host

E. Device

70-098.02.05.004

Which installation methods are valid when installing a modem in Windows 98? (Choose all that apply.)

A. Using the Modems option in Control Panel.

B. Typing **modemdetect** at the Start menu's run line.

C. Adding a modem though the Add New Hardware option in Control Panel.

D. Plugging in your Plug and Play modem and letting Windows 98 connect to it.

E. Running a communications application that causes Window 98 to prompt you to install a modem.

70-098.02.05.005

What are the characteristics of the Windows 98 printing subsystem? (Choose three.)

A. Supports IEEE 1394

B. Supports bidirectional communication

C. Supports Extended Capabilities Port devices

D. Outputs to all non-PostScript printer spools as raw printer data

E. Outputs to all PostScript printer spools as PostScript-language raw printer data

F. Supports only extended capability devices connected to an Extended Capabilities Port

70-098.02.05.003

What are the three types of USB components? (Choose three.)

▶ **Correct Answers: A, D, and E**

    A. **Correct.** A hub is one of the three types of USB components.

    B. **Incorrect.** A unit is not a USB component type.

    C. **Incorrect.** A hub provides ports, but a port is not considered a USB component type.

    D. **Correct.** A host, which is also known as the root, is one of the three types of USB components.

    E. **Correct.** A device is one of the three types of USB components.

70-098.02.05.004

Which installation methods are valid when installing a modem in Windows 98? (Choose all that apply.)

▶ **Correct Answers: A, C, and E**

    A. **Correct.** You can manually configure a modem through Control Panel.

    B. **Incorrect.** Windows 98 does not support Modemdetect.

    C. **Correct.** The Add New Hardware option can automatically detect a modem on the system.

    D. **Incorrect.** Windows 98 does not currently autodetect Plug and Play modems.

    E. **Correct.** If an application requests a modem, and Windows 98 does not currently have one configured, the system will prompt you to begin the steps for installing a modem.

70-098.02.05.005

What are the characteristics of the Windows 98 printing subsystem? (Choose three.)

▶ **Correct Answers: B, C, and E**

    A. **Incorrect.** While Windows 98 supports the IEEE 1394 bus, this is not part of the Windows printing subsystem.

    B. **Correct.** Windows 98 provides support for bidirectional communication, such as a printer returning an "out of paper" message to Windows.

    C. **Correct.** Windows 98 supports ECP for high-speed printing.

    D. **Incorrect.** Windows 98 outputs enhanced metafile (EMF) data to all non-PostScript printers.

    E. **Correct.** Windows 98 will output raw EPS data to PostScript printers.

    F. **Incorrect.** You can connect ECP and non-ECP devices to the port.

70-098.02.05.006

Windows 98 supports multiple displays. What are the requirements for a secondary monitor? (Choose three.)

A. It must support ECP.

B. It must be either a PCI or an Extended Industry Standard Architecture (EISA) device.

C. It must be either a PCI or an Accelerated Graphics Port (AGP) device.

D. It must be able to run in GUI mode or without using VGA resources.

E. It must have a Windows 98 driver that allows it to be a secondary display adapter.

70-098.02.05.007

How do you configure Windows 98 to use a secondary display adapter after it has been installed in the computer?

A. Windows 98 will automatically detect it.

B. Windows 98 will run the Add New Hardware Wizard.

C. Windows 98 will allow you to activate it after it has restarted.

D. Windows 98 will allow you to configure the secondary adapter card after it has restarted.

70-098.02.05.008

Which Windows 98 feature allows future versions of Windows, such as Windows 2000 Workstation, to share common drivers between operating systems?

A. Win32 Driver Model

B. Windows Universal Driver

C. Hardware Abstraction Layer

D. Advanced Configuration and Power Interface

70-098.02.05.006

Windows 98 supports multiple displays. What are the requirements for a secondary monitor? (Choose three.)

▶ **Correct Answers: C, D, and E**

   A. **Incorrect.** The secondary monitor does not have to support ECP.

   B. **Incorrect.** The secondary monitor cannot be EISA-compliant.

   C. **Correct.** Both PCI and AGP devices are supported.

   D. **Correct.** The secondary monitor cannot use VGA resources.

   E. **Correct.** A special Windows 98 driver is required to support multiple monitors.

70-098.02.05.007

How do you configure Windows 98 to use a secondary display adapter after it has been installed in the computer?

▶ **Correct Answer: A**

   A. **Correct.** A key feature to Windows 98's support for Multiple Display Support is its autodetect capabilities.

   B. **Incorrect.** Windows 98 autodetects additional monitors, so the Add New Hardware Wizard is not required.

   C. **Incorrect.** Windows 98 does not have to be restarted to support a secondary monitor.

   D. **Incorrect.** Windows 98 does not have to be restarted to support a secondary monitor.

70-098.02.05.008

Which Windows 98 feature allows future versions of Windows, such as Windows 2000 Workstation, to share common drivers between operating systems?

▶ **Correct Answer: A**

   A. **Correct.** The Win32 Driver Model has been introduced in Windows 98.

   B. **Incorrect.** Windows Universal Driver is not supported by Windows 98.

   C. **Incorrect.** Windows 98 does not support the Hardware Abstraction Layer.

   D. **Incorrect.** Advanced Configuration and Power Interface allows for a standard way to control power management and has nothing to do with future driver architecture.

Further Reading

Microsoft Windows 98 Training Kit. Complete Lesson 2, "Windows 98 Features," of Chapter 1, "The Windows 98 Operating System." In this lesson, the various hardware standards supported by Windows 98 are discussed. OnNow, USB, and Multiple Display Support are described.

Microsoft Windows 98 Training Kit. Complete Lesson 2, "Using OnNow Power Management," of Chapter 4, "Windows 98 Hardware Support." In this lesson, the system requirements to support OnNow are discussed. In addition, you will learn how to configure power management in Windows 98.

Microsoft Windows 98 Training Kit. Complete Lesson 3, "Supporting Universal Serial Bus Devices," of Chapter 4, "Windows 98 Hardware Support." In this lesson, you will learn about the USB topology and how to install and configure USB-compliant devices.

Microsoft Windows 98 Training Kit. Complete Lesson 4, "Supporting IEEE 1394 Serial Bus Devices," of Chapter 4, "Windows 98 Hardware Support." In this lesson, the IEEE 1394 standard is described and you will learn how to install an IEEE 1394 device.

Microsoft Windows 98 Training Kit. Complete Lesson 5, "Multiple Display Support," of Chapter 4, "Windows 98 Hardware Support." In this lesson, the various uses for Multiple Display Support are discussed. You will also learn how to configure multiple monitors and troubleshoot potential problems.

Microsoft Windows 98 Training Kit. Complete Lesson 1, "The Windows 98 Print Subsystem," of Chapter 8, "Supporting Local Printers in Windows 98." In this lesson, the Windows 98 printing subsystem is described. You will also learn about ECP and the benefits of deferred printing.

Microsoft Windows 98 Training Kit. Complete Lesson 2, "Installing a Local Printer," of Chapter 8, "Supporting Local Printers in Windows 98." In this lesson, you will learn how to manually install a local printer.

Microsoft Windows 98 Training Kit. Complete Lesson 3, "Configuring and Managing a Local Printer," of Chapter 8, "Supporting Local Printers in Windows 98." In this lesson, you will learn how to configure and manage local printers.

Microsoft Windows 98 Training Kit. Complete Lesson 1, "Setting Up Dial-Up Networking," of Chapter 18, "Implementing Dial-Up Networking in Windows 98." In this lesson, configuring Dial-Up Networking and the necessary hardware components, such as a modem or ISDN device, is discussed.

Microsoft Windows 98 Training Kit. Complete Lesson 2, "Configuring Dial-Up Networking Clients," of Chapter 18, "Implementing Dial-Up Networking in Windows 98." In this lesson, you will learn how to configure dial-up servers and the required protocols, create a modem script, use a Multilink connection, and use virtual private networking. You will also see how to use a direct cable connection to connect two local computers.

Windows 98 Accelerated MCSE Study Guide. Read Chapter 11, "Printing," to learn more about how Windows 98 supports printer devices.

OBJECTIVE 2.6

Install and configure Microsoft Backup.

Included in Windows 98 is the Microsoft Backup utility. Microsoft Backup is designed for single workstation backups. It supports a variety of hardware and media types, including:

- QIC-80

- TR1, 2, 3, 4

- Digital Audio Tape (DAT)

- DC 6000

- 8mm

- Digital Linear Tape (DLT)

- Removable media, such as floppy disks, Iomega Jaz, or Syquest cartridges

Support has been provided for parallel, IDE/ATAPI, and SCSI devices. However, Microsoft Backup does not support the QIC-40 format. Since this utility is not installed by default, you will need to use Add/Remove Programs in Control Panel before you can back up files. Microsoft Backup is located in the Disk Tools component of Windows 98 and requires at least 5.2 MB of hard drive space.

Once installed, Microsoft Backup can be run using the Backup Wizard. However, you can use Microsoft Backup without the wizard.

To successfully answer the questions for this objective, refer to the Glossary in this book for a definition of the following key term.

Key Term

- Backup device

70-098.02.06.001

A Windows 95 computer has been upgraded to Windows 98. You want to install Microsoft Backup to use with your QIC-40 tape drive. You notice there is no driver that supports your tape device. What should you do?

A. Use the QIC-80 driver.

B. Use the Windows 95 driver.

C. Get an updated driver from the manufacturer.

D. Use the Add New Hardware Wizard and it will install the best driver.

E. Windows 98 does not support QIC-40. You will have to upgrade your tape drive.

70-098.02.06.002

You need a backup system that will meet the following requirements:

1. Restores Windows 95 backups

2. Restores MS-DOS 6.2 backups

3. Backs up to a QIC-40 tape

4. Uses a wizard to maintain current backups

5. Supports DAT drives

If you use Windows 98 Microsoft Backup, which of these requirements are met? (Choose three.)

A. Support for DAT drives

B. Backs up to a QIC-40 tape

C. Restores Windows 95 backups

D. Restores MS-DOS 6.2 backups

E. Uses a wizard to maintain current backups

70-098.02.06.001

A Windows 95 computer has been upgraded to Windows 98. You want to install Microsoft Backup to use with your QIC-40 tape drive. You notice there is no driver that supports your tape device. What should you do?

▶ **Correct Answer: E**

A. **Incorrect.** The QIC-80 drivers will not support the QIC-40 format.

B. **Incorrect.** The Windows 95 driver will not work with Windows 98.

C. **Incorrect.** There are no drivers available because Windows 98 does not support QIC-40.

D. **Incorrect.** Since Windows 98 does not support QIC-40, there are no compatible drivers.

E. **Correct.** Unfortunately, Windows 98 offers no support for the QIC-40 format.

70-098.02.06.002

You need a backup system that will meet the following requirements:

1. Restores Windows 95 backups

2. Restores MS-DOS 6.2 backups

3. Backs up to a QIC-40 tape

4. Uses a wizard to maintain current backups

5. Supports DAT drives

If you use Windows 98 Microsoft Backup, which of these requirements are met? (Choose three.)

▶ **Correct Answers: A, C, and D**

A. **Correct.** Windows 98 supports the DAT format.

B. **Incorrect.** Windows 98 does not support the QIC-40 format.

C. **Correct.** Windows 98 supports restoring Windows 95 backups.

D. **Correct.** Windows 98 supports restoring MS-DOS backups.

E. **Incorrect.** Windows 98 Backup does not include wizard support for managing backups.

70-098.02.06.003

Your customer wants to use Microsoft Backup to archive files on a Windows 98 computer that contains all the company's accounting records. She does not mind taking some time to back up every day, but wants to be able to restore files efficiently. Which backup method should she use?

A. Perform a full backup every day. To restore, use the last full backup.

B. Perform a full backup on Mondays and then perform an incremental backup on the remaining days of the week. To restore, use the last full backup and the last incremental.

C. Perform a full backup on Mondays, and then perform a differential backup on the remaining days of the week. To restore, use the last full backup and the last differential backup.

70-098.02.06.004

You receive a new driver for your tape device and need to install it in your computer. Which Control Panel utility can you use to install the new driver?

A. Users

B. System

C. Backup

D. Accessories

E. Tape Devices

70-098.02.06.003

Your customer wants to use Microsoft Backup to archive files on a Windows 98 computer that contains all the company's accounting records. She does not mind taking some time to back up every day, but wants to be able to restore files efficiently. Which backup method should she use?

▶ **Correct Answer: C**

A. **Incorrect.** A complete backup every day would be inefficient since not all the data will have changed from the previous day. She should consider using the differential backup methodology.

B. **Incorrect.** Using an incremental methodology, she would not be creating the most efficient use of her time. If she is willing to make a backup each night, she should consider using differential backups.

C. **Correct.** This would be the most efficient solution for her backup needs. A full backup and differential backups will reduce the amount of time spent each night making the day's backup archive.

70-098.02.06.004

You receive a new driver for your tape device and need to install it in your computer. Which Control Panel utility can you use to install the new driver?

▶ **Correct Answer: B**

A. **Incorrect.** You do not configure tape devices under Users.

B. **Correct.** You can update existing devices under System.

C. **Incorrect.** Backup does not provide the ability to update drivers.

D. **Incorrect.** There is no Accessories entry in Control Panel.

E. **Incorrect.** The Tape Devices utility does not provide the ability to update drivers.

Further Reading

Microsoft Windows 98 Resource Kit. Read pages 1269–1274 to learn more about installing and using Microsoft Backup.

Windows 98 Accelerated MCSE Study Guide. Read Chapter 5, "Disk Management," to learn more about the backup features included in Windows 98.

Configuring and Managing Resource Access

Windows 98 allows you to access network resources on other computers. In addition, you can configure Windows 98 to allow users across the network to access your resources. These resources include both local printers as well as local files. For this objective, you will need to understand how to configure local printers and make them available for network use.

Depending on whether you have a Windows NT server, or Novell server, available to authenticate users, you will have to decide to use share-level access or user-level access. User-level access is the most secure. For the exam, you will need to understand when to use which security implementation and how to use them effectively. For example, be sure to know the difference between full access and read-only access, and how to configure each when using share-level access.

This objective domain also covers implementing profiles and policies. By using these, either separately or together, you will be able to better control how users interact with the system. This can reduce help desk calls and administration costs. There is also an objective that covers backing up and restoring data. Be sure to know how to install the Microsoft Backup utility and how to use it with and without the included wizard.

Tested Skills and Suggested Practices

The skills you need to successfully master the Configuring and Managing Resource Access Objective Domain on the exam include:

- **Implementing share-level and user-level security.**

    - Practice 1: Create a share on a folder that controls access based on share-level security. You do this by configuring a password on the share. Any user on the network who knows the password will be able to access the files in this folder.

▪ Practice 2: With a Windows NT server on the network, add the Windows 98 computer to the domain and configure a shared folder to use user-level security. You do this by allowing specific users or groups access to the files in the folder. The Windows NT server will provide a list of available users and groups.

■ **Implementing system policies.**

▪ Practice 1: Use System Policy Editor to create a policy based on a user account. Log on to Windows 98 using this account to verify the settings.

▪ Practice 2: With a Windows NT server available, create a system policy based on a group. Log on to Windows 98 with a user account that is in this group to verify the settings.

■ **Implementing user profiles.**

▪ Practice 1: Using Control Panel, enable unique user profiles. Log on to Windows 98 with two different user names to verify that the desktop configurations are maintained from one logon to another.

▪ Practice 2: Configure the user profiles to support roaming users. This will require a Windows NT or NetWare server to store the user profile files.

■ **Configuring a local printer.**

▪ Practice 1: Connect a printer to a Windows 98 computer and configure the appropriate driver.

▪ Practice 2: Share the printer for network use. Try connecting to this printer and print a test page.

■ **Using Microsoft Backup.**

▪ Practice 1: Manually install Microsoft Backup on a Windows 98 computer.

▪ Practice 2: Share the printer for network use. Try connecting to this printer and printing a test page.

■ **Managing hardware profiles.**

▪ Practice 1: Using a laptop and a docking station, allow Windows 98 to automatically create a "docked" and an "undocked" profile.

▪ Practice 2: Using two different logon accounts, create custom hardware profiles for each. Test the results by logging onto Windows 98 with each account and verifying which hardware devices are available for each user.

OBJECTIVE 3.1

Assign access permissions for shared folders in a Microsoft environment and a mixed Microsoft and NetWare environment.

Objective 3.1 includes three methods to consider when assigning access to shared folders:

- Passwords

- User permissions

- Group permissions

In order for Windows 98 to share file resources, the appropriate Client for Microsoft Networks and/or Client for NetWare Networks must be installed. In addition, File and Printer Sharing needs to be installed and configured based on the network type you are using, Microsoft or Novell. Once these network components have been configured, you can allow users on the network to share your files. However, you will probably want to restrict, or limit, access to these files. How you do this will depend heavily on what network server resources are available.

The easiest way to protect your files would be to assign a password based on read-only or full access. If a user does not have one of these passwords, he will not be able to access the files. Unfortunately, any user who knows the password will have access to the file. Other than controlling who knows the password, you cannot restrict access based on user name. This security scheme is designed for use in a peer-to-peer network and provides limited control.

A more secure technique is to implement user-level security. With user-level security, you can control by user name who has read-only access, full access, or no access. If you want to implement user-level security, Windows 98 must be part of a Windows NT or NetWare network that includes a server that can authenticate user names.

However, in large organizations, it is not realistic to manage the users who have access to your shared folders on an individual basis. For instance, as employees are added to the company, or leave the company, you would have to manually update the access list. By using predefined group names, you can effectively add or remove users based on the groups they belong to. This makes it easier to control large numbers of users who might need access to your shares.

To successfully answer the questions for this objective, you need a firm understanding of several key terms. For definitions of these terms, refer to the Glossary in this book.

Key Terms

- Domain

- NetBEUI

- Network protocol

- Peer-to-peer network

- Share-level security

- TCP/IP

- User-level security

70-098.03.01.001

You would like to share a folder on your Windows 98 computer with certain domain users. The data changes frequently, and you want to make the data available to the users immediately. Which methods should you choose if you also want a high degree of security? (Choose two.)

A. Apply user-level security on the Windows 98 computer.

B. Use share-level security and inform only the appropriate users of the password.

C. Copy the folder to the server and have the network administrator apply security.

D. Choose a security provider to validate users when they attempt to access your shared folder.

70-098.03.01.002

How can you allow certain users to alter a shared file and give remaining users read access to the file on a peer-to-peer network? (Choose two.)

A. Select Read-only as the Access Type.

B. Select Full as the Access Type.

C. Choose user-level security from Control Panel's Network utility.

D. Select Depends on Password as the Access Type for share-level access.

E. Create a password for the Read-only users and a different password for the Full access users.

70-098.03.01.001

You would like to share a folder on your Windows 98 computer with certain domain users. The data changes frequently, and you want to make the data available to the users immediately. Which methods should you choose if you also want a high degree of security? (Choose two.)

▶ **Correct Answers: A and D**

A. **Correct.** User-level security provides the most control over who has access to the files. Share-level security does not require the user to be authenticated first and is therefore less secure.

B. **Incorrect.** Share-level security, which is more secure than no security, only requires users to know a general password. Any user who knows the password can have access. User-level security provides a higher level of security because you can control who has access to the files on an individual basis.

C. **Incorrect.** While this solution may be more secure than share-level security, it would require changes to the files to be saved each time to the network. This would not provide the fastest updates for the users.

D. **Correct.** In combination with user-level security, a security provider, such as Windows NT, will authenticate the users and only allow users with permission to access the files.

70-098.03.01.002

How can you allow certain users to alter a shared file and give remaining users read access to the file on a peer-to-peer network? (Choose two.)

▶ **Correct Answers: D and E**

A. **Incorrect.** By selecting Read-only, all users will have only this access. Thus, no changes could be made to the files.

B. **Incorrect.** Setting permission to Full Control would give all users the ability to edit the files. Thus, no users would only have Read-only access—they would all have full editing capabilities.

C. **Incorrect.** User-level security requires a server to authenticate users. Since this is a peer-to-peer environment, only share-level security is available.

D. **Correct.** Since this is a peer-to-peer environment, to secure access, you must assign passwords to the share.

E. **Correct.** Once passwords have been enabled on the share, you need to specify different passwords for each level of access. Those who have Full Control can edit, while those with Read-only access will only be able to view the documents.

70-098.03.01.003

Your Windows 98 computer is logged on to the corporate domain. You want to share a folder with a group of users in the accounting department. What is the most secure way to share the folder?

A. Use the Windows NT server as a security provider and use share-level access control.

B. Use share-level access control and set a password for the folder for the accounting users.

C. Use share-level access control, use the Depends on Password option, and grant the users in the accounting department access.

D. Use user-level access control, use the Windows NT domain controller as your security provider, and grant access to the accounting group.

70-098.03.01.003

Your Windows 98 computer is logged on to the corporate domain. You want to share a folder with a group of users in the accounting department. What is the most secure way to share the folder?

▶ **Correct Answer: D**

A. **Incorrect.** If you are using Windows NT to authenticate users, share-level security will not provide the highest level of security. Share-level should only be used in a peer-to-peer workgroup where no server is available.

B. **Incorrect.** Since Windows NT is available, you do not have to use the less secure share-level security.

C. **Incorrect.** Even by specifying a password using share-level security, user-level security should be implemented for the highest level of control. Since there is a Windows NT server available to authenticate users, user-level security can be implemented.

D. **Correct.** Using Windows NT groups, user-level security can be implemented and the accounting group can be assigned rights to the share. If the group does not already exist, a Windows NT administrator will have to first create the group. While you could add each individual user from the accounting department, a Windows NT group would be more efficient for this task.

70-098.03.01.004

You create a share named ACCOUNTING and assign passwords to the share. You give both John and Jane a password to the share. John can access the share and change information on the share. Jane can read the share, but cannot change information in the folder.

Why can't Jane change information on the share in this share-level security environment? (Choose all that apply.)

A. Jane typed in an incorrect password.

B. Jane has the Read-only password.

C. John has the Read-only password.

D. John has the password for Full access.

E. Jane is not a member of the appropriate group.

F. Jane has the password for Full access.

70-098.03.01.004

You create a share named ACCOUNTING and assign passwords to the share. You give both John and Jane a password to the share. John can access the share and change information on the share. Jane can read the share, but cannot change information in the folder.

Why can't Jane change information on the share in this share-level security environment? (Choose all that apply.)

▶ **Correct Answers: B and D**

A. **Incorrect.** Had Jane entered an invalid password, she would not be able to access the files to edit or to read. Since she is able to gain Read access to files, we know that she entered the Read-only password correctly.

B. **Correct.** Users who can only view, but not change, files in a share-level protected folder must be using a valid Read-only password. Had they used the Full access password, they would automatically be able to edit the files.

C. **Incorrect.** Since John can edit the files, he must be using the Full access password. Had he used the Read-only password, he would not be given permission to change the files.

D. **Correct.** Only users who have the Full access password can view and edit files in a folder that has share-level security enabled. Unfortunately, all users who know this password will be given access to the files. Share-level security does not consider the user name, only the password provided.

E. **Incorrect.** In a share-level security environment, user name and groups are irrelevant. Only entering the appropriate password is required to access files. This is the main limitation to using this security strategy.

F. **Incorrect.** If Jane had the Full access password, she would be able to edit the files. Unfortunately, all users who know this password will be given access to the files. Share-level security does not consider the user name, only the password provided.

70-098.03.01.005

Examine the Windows 98 configuration shown below.

If you share a folder as DOCUMENTS, which network operating systems will be able to access this share? (Choose all that apply.)

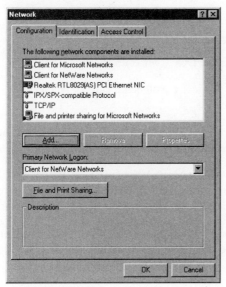

A. Windows 95

B. NetWare 4.1

C. Windows NT Server 4.0

D. Windows for Workgroups

E. Windows NT Workstation 4.0

70-098.03.01.005

Examine the Windows 98 configuration shown on the previous page.

If you share a folder as DOCUMENTS, which network operating systems will be able to access this share? (Choose all that apply.)

▶ **Correct Answers: A, C, and E**

A. **Correct.** Windows 95 supports both NetBEUI and TCP/IP. Therefore, with the current network protocols, a Windows 95 client would be able to access the DOCUMENTS share.

B. **Incorrect.** Since no NetWare-compatible protocols or services have been installed, NetWare clients would not be able to access the DOCUMENT share.

C. **Correct.** Windows NT Server supports both NetBEUI and TCP/IP. Therefore, with the current network protocols, a Windows NT server would be able to access the DOCUMENTS share.

D. **Incorrect.** Although Windows for Workgroups supports both NetBEUI and TCP/IP, it does not support long filenames. Therefore, a share with the name of DOCUMENTS cannot be accessed by Windows for Workgroups clients.

E. **Correct.** Windows NT Workstation supports both NetBEUI and TCP/IP. Therefore, with the current network protocols, a Windows NT workstation would be able to access the DOCUMENTS share.

Further Reading

Microsoft Windows 98 Training Kit. Complete Lesson 2, "Sharing Windows 98 Resources," of Chapter 12, "Configuring Windows 98 for Use on a Network." In this lesson, you will learn how to install and configure Client for Microsoft Networks and File and Printer Sharing.

Microsoft Windows 98 Training Kit. Complete Lesson 2, "Logging on to a NetWare Server," of Chapter 14, "Using Windows 98 on a Novell Network." In this lesson, configuring IPX/SPX and the NetWare network components are discussed.

Microsoft Windows 98 Training Kit. Complete Lesson 4, "Sharing Resources with NetWare Users," of Chapter 14, "Using Windows 98 on a Novell Network." In this lesson, you will learn how to install and configure Client for NetWare Networks and File and Printer Sharing.

Windows 98 Accelerated MCSE Study Guide. Read Chapter 9, "Network Security," to learn more about user-level and share-level security.

OBJECTIVE 3.2

Create, share, and monitor resources including remote computers and network printers.

Connecting to other computers and accessing their resources is critical in an enterprise environment. Windows 98 provides a number of features to help users get the most out of network access. Windows 98 can share resources with NetWare servers and clients the same way as with a Microsoft network. The configuration process, however, differs for NetWare, and the access control level is limited to user-level access. When you use File and Printer Sharing for NetWare Networks to share resources with NetWare clients, your computer appears to a NetWare server as a NetWare client. Objective 3.2 focuses on connecting a Windows 98 client to shared resources on both a Microsoft and NetWare network.

To successfully answer the questions for this objective, you need a firm understanding of several key terms. For definitions of these terms, refer to the Glossary in this book.

Key Terms

- Share-level security

- User-level security

70-098.03.02.001

How can you connect to a Microsoft print server from a Windows 98 computer? (Choose all that apply.)

A. Type the path of the print server in the Run dialog box on the Start menu.

B. Use the Add Network Printer Wizard and type the name of the print server.

C. Use the Add Printer Wizard and browse or type the path of the print server.

D. Open the print server's print queue using Network Neighborhood or Windows Explorer.

70-098.03.02.002

What must occur before a Windows 98 workstation can connect using Point and Print to a NetWare 3.12 print server? (Choose two.)

A. The printer drivers must be installed locally.

B. Client for NetWare Networks must be installed locally.

C. Services for NetWare Directory Services must be installed locally.

D. A Supervisor of the NetWare print server must store the printer driver files in the bindery.

E. A Supervisor of the NetWare print server must add the computer name of the Windows 98 computer to the bindery.

70-098.03.02.001

How can you connect to a Microsoft print server from a Windows 98 computer? (Choose all that apply.)

▶ **Correct Answers: A, C, and D**

   A. **Correct.** As long as the Windows 98 client has the appropriate network access, a print server can be accessed by entering the path to the printer, such as \\printsrv\printername.

   B. **Incorrect.** There is no Add Network Printer Wizard included in Windows 98. The Add Printer Wizard supports both local and network printers.

   C. **Correct.** Using the Add Printer Wizard, you can manually connect to network printers. You can also configure local printers using this wizard.

   D. **Correct.** You can locate and access a print server's queue in Network Neighborhood or the Windows Explorer in much the same way as you do when using the Run command prompt.

70-098.03.02.002

What must occur before a Windows 98 workstation can connect using Point and Print to a NetWare 3.12 print server? (Choose two.)

▶ **Correct Answers: B and D**

   A. **Incorrect.** When connecting to a NetWare printer, the drivers are stored on the NetWare server.

   B. **Correct.** To access any NetWare resource, the Windows 98 client must have Client for NetWare Networks installed. This will automatically install IPX/SPX if this protocol is not already available.

   C. **Incorrect.** Since we are only connecting to a shared printer, NDS is not required on the Windows 98 client.

   D. **Correct.** Windows 98 does not install the printer driver for a NetWare-based network printer. Instead, the NetWare server must make the drivers available to be used when a printing request is submitted from a client, such as Windows 98.

   E. **Incorrect.** The name of the Windows 98 client is not required in order to access a shared NetWare printer. Only the printer drivers must be stored in the bindery.

70-098.03.02.003

You want to share your printer with other users in your Windows 98 workgroup. How do the users access the drivers for your printer?

A. You must create a hidden share for your printer drivers.

B. Users who want to use your printer must install the drivers locally first.

C. Share the folder where the drivers reside and have the users copy them to their C:\Windows\System folder.

D. When users connect to your printer, the drivers are copied to their local computer's C:\Windows\System folder automatically.

70-098.03.02.003

You want to share your printer with other users in your Windows 98 workgroup. How do the users access the drivers for your printer?

▶ **Correct Answer: D**

   A. **Incorrect.** Since the printer drivers are automatically installed when a user connects to the shared printer, creating a hidden share will have no effect for the users.

   B. **Incorrect.** The printer drivers will be installed and configured for the user when they connect to the printer. Therefore, they do not have to first manually install the drivers locally.

   C. **Incorrect.** Printer drivers must be registered with Windows 98 and cannot just be copied to the local \Windows\System folder. When a user connects to the network printer, the drivers will be installed and configured automatically.

   D. **Correct.** Since Windows 98 will automatically configure the drivers, you only have to connect to the network printer. No additional setup is required.

Further Reading

Microsoft Windows 98 Training Kit. Complete Lesson 2, "Sharing Windows 98 Resources," of Chapter 12, "Configuring Windows 98 for Use on a Network." In this lesson, installing and configuring Client for Microsoft Networks and File and Printer sharing are discussed.

Microsoft Windows 98 Training Kit. Complete Lesson 3, "Using Windows NT Network Resources," of Chapter 13, "Using Windows 98 on a Windows NT Network." In this lesson, you will learn how to connect to a Windows NT server and access a Windows NT print server. You will also enable user-level security and assign folder permissions.

Microsoft Windows 98 Training Kit. Complete Lesson 4, "Sharing Resources with NetWare Users," of Chapter 14, "Using Windows 98 on a Novell Network." In this lesson, you will learn how to install and configure Client for NetWare Networks and File and Printer Sharing.

Windows 98 Accelerated MCSE Study Guide. Read Chapter 11, "Printing," to learn more about sharing a printer on a network and accessing remote printers.

OBJECTIVE 3.3

Set up user environments by using user profiles and system policies.

Windows 98 not only allows users to customize their desktops, but it will also remember one user's configuration versus another. These settings are saved in a user profile. In addition, administrators can control what applications and interface options are presented to the user through policies. By combining profiles and policies, you can implement complete control of the user's system. This is especially important in a roaming user environment. For larger organizations, policies can also be assigned by group. To implement system policies, Windows 98 includes System Policy Editor.

To successfully answer the questions for this objective, you need a firm understanding of several key terms. For definitions of these terms, refer to the Glossary in this book.

Key Terms

- Group policies

- Hardware profile

- User profile

70-098.03.03.001

You set up group policies, but they are not enforced for some users when they log on. What could be causing this problem? (Choose all that apply.)

A. The users have individual profiles.

B. The users are not members of the group.

C. The client computers do not have user profiles enabled.

D. The client computers are not configured for group policy support.

70-098.03.03.002

Users on your network have been modifying their computer configuration by booting into safe mode and changing their system settings. This causes computer malfunctions and an increase in the number of help desk calls. Which actions can prevent users from modifying their computer configurations? (Choose two.)

A. Modify the MSDOS.SYS file so the user cannot avoid starting Windows 98.

B. Change the computer's CMOS settings so the user cannot boot from a floppy disk.

C. Convert the disk drive to FAT32, format it, and configure it for user-level security.

D. Modify the registry setting named Require Validation By Network For Windows Access to require booting only into Windows.

70-098.03.03.001

You set up group policies, but they are not enforced for some users when they log on. What could be causing this problem? (Choose all that apply.)

▶ **Correct Answers: B, C, and D**

    A. **Incorrect.** Enabling user profiles is required for a policy to be implemented. Therefore, having an individual profile would not prevent a policy from being used.

    B. **Correct.** If the user is not a member of the group, the associated policy will not be enforced for that user.

    C. **Correct.** User profiles must be enabled on the client computer before a group policy will be enforced.

    D. **Correct.** If group policies are not installed through the Add/Remove Programs utility in Control Panel, they cannot be used.

70-098.03.03.002

Users on your network have been modifying their computer configuration by booting into safe mode and changing their system settings. This causes computer malfunctions and an increase in the number of help desk calls. Which actions can prevent users from modifying their computer configurations? (Choose two.)

▶ **Correct Answer: A and B**

    A. **Correct.** The hidden MSDOS.SYS file contains boot information for Windows 98. If you set the BootDelay option to 0, users will not be able to interrupt the Windows 98 startup.

    B. **Correct.** By restricting the user's ability to boot from a floppy, you can further limit access to Windows 98 safe mode. Consider locking CMOS with a password so the user cannot enter CMOS and re-enable the ability to boot from a floppy.

    C. **Incorrect.** Formatting the drive will not affect whether the user can access Windows 98 safe mode. The MSDOS.SYS file controls this ability.

    D. **Incorrect.** No registry settings need to be modified to control access to safe mode.

70-098.03.03.003

You are the system administrator for an organization running more than 2,000 Windows 98 client computers on a Windows NT domain. System policies were recently implemented on these computers. Logon validation requests are very slow and some users are complaining.

What is causing this problem and how can it be solved?

A. You have included too many groups in the policy file on the servers. Edit the file and remove some of the groups.

B. Load balancing is not enabled in the policy file and consequently all clients are downloading the settings from the Primary Domain Controller. Enable load balancing.

C. Since users cannot change mandatory policies, the changes will not be written to the server, thereby improving performance. Change the policies to mandatory policies.

D. The computers are not finding the policy file because Directory Replication is not working properly on the Windows NT servers. Configure replication on all the domain controllers.

70-098.03.03.004

Your work requires you to be in the office and out in the field. Your primary computer is a Pentium-based laptop. The laptop has a modem and a network card installed in it. You need to set up the computer so you do not have to reconfigure it every time you switch from the network at the office to dial-up access when in the field.

What should you do?

A. Create a hardware profile named field and remove the network card on the profile. Create a hardware profile named office and remove the modem on the profile.

B. Create a hardware profile named office and remove the network card on the profile. Create a hardware profile named field and remove the modem on the profile.

C. Create a hardware profile named office and disable the network card on the profile. Create a hardware profile named field and disable the modem on the profile.

D. Create a hardware profile named field and disable the network card on the profile. Create a hardware profile named office and disable the modem on the profile.

70-098.03.03.003

You are the system administrator for an organization running more than 2,000 Windows 98 client computers on a Windows NT domain. System policies were recently implemented on these computers. Logon validation requests are very slow and some users are complaining.

What is causing this problem and how can it be solved?

▶ **Correct Answer: B**

A. **Incorrect.** Policy files can support an unlimited number of users, groups, or computers. However, if there is a large number of users logging on, the process can slow down. Therefore, load balancing should be enabled to better balance network resources.

B. **Correct.** Load balancing will help ensure network efficiency when policies have been enabled. If load balancing is enabled, all domain controllers must have the same copy of the policy file. You can ensure this by enabling the Directory Replication service.

C. **Incorrect.** Policies are always mandatory. Therefore, if logon processes are taking too long, you should be sure to enable load balancing across the various domain controllers on the network.

D. **Incorrect.** While Directory Replication will ensure that the same policy file exists on all domain controllers, it is not required. Load balancing must be enabled to provide the most efficient use of network resources. Directory Replication will simply help manage the policy files on the network.

70-098.03.03.004

Your work requires you to be in the office and out in the field. Your primary computer is a Pentium-based laptop. The laptop has a modem and a network card installed in it. You need to set up the computer so you do not have to reconfigure it every time you switch from the network at the office to dial-up access when in the field.

What should you do?

▶ **Correct Answer: D**

A. **Incorrect.** If a device is removed, it must be reinstalled before you can use it. Therefore, disabling is a better choice since you will be switching between the field and the office.

B. **Incorrect.** Removing a device that will be needed is not optimal since it will have to be reinstalled when you return to the office (or the field). In addition, you would not want to remove the network card from the office profile since that is when you'll need it.

C. **Incorrect.** Although disabling a device is the best way to solve this problem, you would not want to disable the network card while in the office. Instead, you would disable the modem in the office profile and the network card in the field profile.

D. **Correct.** Disabling the unneeded device is preferable to removing because, by changing profiles, the system will have the appropriate devices configured and ready to work properly. If you were to remove the device, it would have to be reinstalled when needed.

70-098.03.03.005

Examine the Passwords Properties dialog box below. You are setting up user profiles and have configured them as seen in the exhibit.

Which settings for the profile will be created?

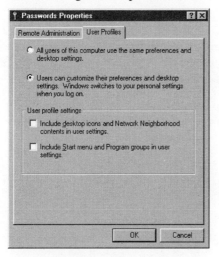

A. No settings will be created.

B. User-specific registry settings.

C. Computer-specific registry settings.

D. Default user profile with desktop settings.

E. Default user profile with Start menu and program groups.

F. Default user profile with Start menu, program groups, and desktop settings.

70-098.03.03.005

Examine the Passwords Properties dialog box shown on the previous page. You are setting up user profiles and have configured them as seen in the exhibit.

Which settings for the profile will be created?

▶ **Correct Answer: B**

A. **Incorrect.** Regardless of which options are selected, there are always settings that will be created. By default, computer-specific settings are saved to the registry. This means that the same settings will be used regardless of the user.

B. **Correct.** Since neither of the User Profile settings have been checked, no default settings will be created. However, since users can customize their settings, registry information will be saved based on the user. This means that when the users log on at a later time, the system will remember their settings automatically.

C. **Incorrect.** Computer-specific settings are the default and would be created if the first option, All Users of This Computer..., were selected. However, since the system will remember each individual user's settings, computer-specific settings are no longer active.

D. **Incorrect.** To create default user settings that include the desktop settings, the first option under User Profile settings would need to be checked. In this case, it is not, so this setting will not be used.

E. **Incorrect.** To create default user settings that include the Start menu and program groups, the second option under User Profile settings would need to be checked. In this case, it is not, so this setting will not be used.

F. **Incorrect.** To create default user settings that include the Start menu, program groups, and desktop settings, both options under User Profile settings would need to be checked. In this case, they are not, so these settings will not be used.

Further Reading

Microsoft Windows 98 Training Kit. Read Chapter 15, "Managing Windows 98 User Profiles," for an overview of how to enable and configure user profiles.

Microsoft Windows 98 Training Kit. Read Chapter 16, "Implementing Windows 98 System Policies," for an overview of how to enable and configure system policies.

Microsoft Windows 98 Training Kit. Read page 412 to learn more about load balancing system policies.

Microsoft Windows 98 Resource Kit. Read pages 194–195 to learn more about the options available in MSDOS.SYS.

Microsoft Windows 98 Resource Kit. Read pages 318–319 to learn more about system policies.

Microsoft Windows 98 Resource Kit. Read page 352 to learn more about troubleshooting group policies.

Windows 98 Accelerated MCSE Study Guide. Read Chapter 10, "Policies and Profiles," to learn more about how Windows 98 supports custom profiles.

OBJECTIVE 3.4

Back up data and restore data.

Using Microsoft Backup, you can back up files and other data. To back up the system registry, Windows 98 includes the Registry Checker program. The Registry Checker runs automatically. However, you can run it manually to force a backup, or restore, of the registry. For this objective, be sure you know how to use Microsoft Backup and how to manually run the Registry Checker.

To successfully answer the questions for this objective, refer to the Glossary in this book for a definition of the following key term.

Key Term

- Removable device

70-098.03.04.001

How is Microsoft Backup used to back up files to a removable device?

A. During the backup, specify the removable device as the target drive.

B. During the backup, specify the file where you need to save the backup.

C. Select the removable device as your backup device in the Microsoft Backup Wizard.

D. Install a driver for the removable device that allows it to function as a backup device.

70-098.03.04.002

When restoring files using Microsoft Backup, which of the following are true ? (Choose two.)

A. You must use the Restore Wizard to restore files.

B. You can restore backups made by the Windows 95 backup program.

C. You can restore files backed up by the MS-DOS 5.1 backup program.

D. Files are restored in their original folder structure unless you choose to restore all files to an alternate location.

70-098.03.04.001

How is Microsoft Backup used to back up files to a removable device?

▶ **Correct Answer: B**

    A. **Incorrect.** When using a removable device, you must specify a file for the backup data. When you do this, you can select the removable drive.

    B. **Correct.** To use a removable device with Microsoft Backup, you will need to specify a file during the backup process. When you do this, select the removable drive as the target file location.

    C. **Incorrect.** You need to specify the file, not the removable device, when backing up.

    D. **Incorrect.** While drivers are normally required for most removable devices, such as Iomega Jaz or Syquest, they do not have to be configured as a backup device.

70-098.03.04.002

When restoring files using Microsoft Backup, which of the following are true ? (Choose two.)

▶ **Correct Answers: B and D**

    A. **Incorrect.** Although the Backup Wizard has been designed to make backing up and restoring data easier, you are not required to use it.

    B. **Correct.** The Windows 98 version of Microsoft Backup program will restore backups that have been created in Windows 95. However, QIC-40 is not supported.

    C. **Incorrect.** Backups created in MS-DOS version 6.x and earlier are not supported by the Microsoft Backup utility included with Windows 98.

    D. **Correct.** By default, files will be restored to their original location. However, you can choose to restore all files to an alternative location.

70-098.03.04.003

Which devices are supported by Windows 98's version of Microsoft Backup? (Choose all that apply.)

A. DAT

B. 8mm

C. QIC-40

D. DC 6000

E. Iomega Jaz drive

70-098.03.04.004

Which names are valid for a backup created with Microsoft Backup? (Choose three.)

A. Backup$

B. <backup>

C. backup-a

D. backup_01

E. Backup|file

F. Backup 1/1/89

0-098.03.04.003

Which devices are supported by Windows 98's version of Microsoft Backup? (Choose all that apply.)

▶ **Correct Answers: A, B, D, and E**

A. **Correct.** Microsoft Backup supports the DAT format.

B. **Correct.** Microsoft Backup supports the 8mm format.

C. **Incorrect.** Microsoft Backup does not support the QIC-40 format.

D. **Correct.** Microsoft Backup supports the DC 6000 format.

E. **Correct.** Microsoft Backup will back up to a removable device, such as the Iomega Jaz.

70-098.03.04.004

Which names are valid for a backup created with Microsoft Backup? (Choose three.)

▶ **Correct Answers: A, C, and D**

A. **Correct.** This name is valid and can be used by Microsoft Backup.

B. **Incorrect.** This name is invalid because you cannot use the < or > signs.

C. **Correct.** This name is valid and can be used by Microsoft Backup.

D. **Correct.** This name is valid and can be used by Microsoft Backup.

E. **Incorrect.** This name is invalid because you cannot use the pipe character (|) in the filename.

F. **Incorrect.** This name is invalid because you cannot use slashes (/) in the filename.

Further Reading

Microsoft Windows 98 Training Kit. Read Chapter 10, "Troubleshooting Windows 98 in a Stand-alone Environment," for an overview on resolving hardware and software conflicts.

Microsoft Windows 98 Resource Kit. Read pages 1455–1457 to learn more about the Registry Checker.

Windows 98 Accelerated MCSE Study Guide. Read Chapter 5, "Disk Management," to learn more about the backup features included in Windows 98.

OBJECTIVE 3.5

Configure hard disks.

The main focus of Objective 3.5 is on using DriveSpace3's compression agent to optimize the amount of space available on a hard drive. Remember, FAT32 file systems cannot be compressed using DriveSpace3. Disk compression shrinks data to reduce the space necessary to store it. Support is provided for partitions that have been compressed with the Windows 95 DriveSpace compression engine. There are four methods of compression, each posing different trade-offs between speed and compression ratio. The four different methods are No Compression, Standard Compression, HiPack, and UltraPack.

This objective also covers managing hard drive partitions. When you set up a new computer system or install a new hard disk, you must prepare the hard disk to store data by first creating one or more partitions and then formatting each partition. Partitioning is the process of establishing one or more isolated sections of mass storage on a hard disk. At a minimum, a hard disk must contain one partition. You create and delete both primary and extended partitions with Fdisk, an MS-DOS utility.

You will also need to know how to enable large drive support, using FAT32, and how to convert a file system to FAT32. Also, be ready to list implications of upgrading to FAT32 or using FAT32 in a dual boot environment.

To successfully answer the questions for this objective, you need a firm understanding of several key terms. For definitions of these terms, refer to the Glossary in this book.

Key Terms

- Compression

- DriveSpace3

- FAT16

- FAT32

70-098.03.05.001

You have 12 Windows 98 computers with 5.7-GB hard drives. You are considering converting the FAT partitions into FAT32 partitions. What are valid reasons to convert a hard drive to FAT32? (Choose two.)

A. You do not want to revert to Windows 95.

B. You need to dual boot between Windows 98 and Windows 95 OSR2.

C. You only have 50 MB of free disk space on your current hard drives.

D. You want an 8-KB cluster on your hard drive instead of 32-KB clusters.

E. You need to dual boot between Windows 98 and Windows NT Workstation 4.0.

70-098.03.05.002

You want to install a new program on your Windows 98 computer, but you do not have enough free disk space. How can you maximize free disk space without adding a hard drive or removing any programs?

A. Use DriveSpace3 to compress the existing files.

B. Create an empty drive using only part of the free space.

C. Create a new compressed drive from free space on the hard disk.

D. Use DriveSpace3 to compress both the existing files and the free disk space.

70-098.03.05.001

You have 12 Windows 98 computers with 5.7-GB hard drives. You are considering converting the FAT partitions into FAT32 partitions. What are valid reasons to convert a hard drive to FAT32? (Choose two.)

▶ **Correct Answers: A and C**

A. **Correct.** If you convert a Windows 98 system to FAT32, you will not be able to revert back to Windows 95. Windows 95 supports only the FAT16 file system.

B. **Incorrect.** Although Windows 95 OSR2 can read a FAT32 file system, you cannot dual boot between Windows 98 and Windows 95.

C. **Correct.** FAT32 uses drive space more efficiently and can therefore provide additional space on a drive.

D. **Incorrect.** FAT32 uses 32-KB clusters, so by upgrading to FAT32 you would be implementing 32-KB, not 8-KB, clusters.

E. **Incorrect.** Windows NT 4 cannot access a FAT32 system. Therefore you would not able to dual boot to Windows NT.

70-098.03.05.002

You want to install a new program on your Windows 98 computer, but you do not have enough free disk space. How can you maximize free disk space without adding a hard drive or removing any programs?

▶ **Correct Answer: D**

A. **Incorrect.** While compressing the existing files will open additional space, the currently available space would not be compressed and therefore would not yield the most available free space.

B. **Incorrect.** By creating a new drive from some of the free space, you will not obtain the most available space. Use DriveSpace3 to compress the entire drive to obtain the most available space.

C. **Incorrect.** By creating a new compressed drive from existing free space, you will not be getting the most available space from the entire hard drive. You should compress the entire drive, including all free space, to obtain the most space available.

D. **Correct.** Only by compressing both the existing files and the currently available space will you be given the most possible free space for additional files or programs.

70-098.03.05.003

You are using DriveSpace3 on your Windows 98 computer. You need to install a program that cannot reside on a compressed drive. The program is 100 MB. The host drive has 10 MB of free space and the Compressed Volume File (CVF) has 200 MB of free disk space.

How must the program be installed to keep the compressed drive intact?

A. This cannot be done without removing the CVF.

B. Create a new drive from the compressed drive with 100 MB of free space, and install the program.

C. Move 100 MB of free space from the CVF to the host drive and install the program on the host drive.

D. Use the LOCK command to enable direct disk access to the compressed drive and install the program on the compressed drive.

70-098.03.05.004

You upgrade from Windows 95 to Windows 98 and save system files during installation. After installing Windows 98, you compress the hard drive using DriveSpace. You want to restore your Windows 95 operating system.

Which command will begin the restoration process?

A. Win95

B. Winundo

C. Winrest

D. Restore95

E. Winundo98

F. Windows 95 cannot be restored.

70-098.03.05.003

You are using DriveSpace3 on your Windows 98 computer. You need to install a program that cannot reside on a compressed drive. The program is 100 MB. The host drive has 10 MB of free space and the Compressed Volume File (CVF) has 200 MB of free disk space.

How must the program be installed to keep the compressed drive intact?

▶ **Correct Answer: C**

    A. **Incorrect.** You do not have to remove the compressed volume to convert some of the compressed space to noncompressed space.

    B. **Incorrect.** If you create a new drive using some of the available compressed space, you still will not be able to install the program. The program requires uncompressed drive space.

    C. **Correct.** Only by moving some of the unused compressed space back to the uncompressed drive will you be able to install the program.

    D. **Incorrect.** Using the LOCK command will not create the additional space required for the application to install successfully.

70-098.03.05.004

You upgrade from Windows 95 to Windows 98 and save system files during installation. After installing Windows 98, you compress the hard drive using DriveSpace. You want to restore your Windows 95 operating system.

Which command will begin the restoration process?

▶ **Correct Answer: F**

    A. **Incorrect.** If you compress a Windows 98 system, you will no longer be able to uninstall and return to a previous operating system. Therefore Win95 will have no effect.

    B. **Incorrect.** If you compress a Windows 98 system, you will no longer be able to uninstall and return to a previous operating system. Therefore Winundo will have no effect.

    C. **Incorrect.** If you compress a Windows 98 system, you will no longer be able to uninstall and return to a previous operating system. Therefore Winrest will have no effect.

    D. **Incorrect.** If you compress a Windows 98 system, you will no longer be able to uninstall and return to a previous operating system. Therefore Restore95 will have no effect.

    E. **Incorrect.** If you compress a Windows 98 system, you will no longer be able to uninstall and return to a previous operating system. Therefore Winundo98 will have no effect.

    F. **Correct.** Once a Windows 98 system has been compressed, it cannot be restored to the previous operating system such as Windows 95.

70-098.03.05.005

How large must a partition be for Windows 98 to convert it from FAT16 to FAT32?

A. 256 MB

B. 512 MB

C. 1024 MB

D. 2048 MB

70-098.03.05.005

How large must a partition be for Windows 98 to convert it from FAT16 to FAT32?

▶ **Correct Answer: B**

A. **Incorrect.** A partition must be at least 512 MB before it can be converted to FAT32. A 256-MB partition is too small and cannot be converted.

B. **Correct.** The minimum partition size is 512 MB.

C. **Incorrect.** The minimum partition size is 512 MB.

D. **Incorrect.** The minimum partition size is 512 MB.

Further Reading

Microsoft Windows 98 Training Kit. Complete Lesson 1, "Partitioning a Hard Disk," of Chapter 3, "Windows 98 File System Support." In this lesson you will learn how to create primary and extended partitions.

Microsoft Windows 98 Training Kit. Complete Lesson 2, "Choosing a File System in Windows 98," of Chapter 3, "Windows 98 File System Support." In this lesson you will learn about the difference between FAT16 and FAT32.

Microsoft Windows 98 Training Kit. Complete Lesson 4, "Implementing Disk Compress," of Chapter 3, "Windows 98 File System Support." In this lesson you will compress drives using DriveSpace3.

Windows 98 Accelerated MCSE Study Guide. Read Chapter 5, "Disk Management," to learn more about how Windows 98 supports hard drives.

Create hardware profiles.

A powerful feature of Windows 98 is the creation and management of hardware profiles. Hardware profiles are particularly useful for laptop owners. For example, you may need one hardware configuration when using your laptop at the office and another configuration when the laptop is being used out of the office. Through the use of profiles, you can enable and disable two devices that conflict but need to reside in the same computer. If you use different profiles, one device will be enabled under one profile, while the other is disabled, and vice versa with a second profile. This eliminates the need to reconfigure, and possibly reinstall, hardware devices. All hardware profile settings are saved in the registry.

To successfully answer the questions for this objective, refer to the Glossary in this book for a definition of the following key term.

Key Term

- Hardware profile

70-098.03.06.001

Steve and John share a Windows 98 computer. The computer has the following components installed in it: a sound card, three video cards, a modem, a parallel Zip drive, a SCSI controller with a hard drive and CD-ROM, and a parallel CD-ROM and disk drive. When setting up the computer, you need the following results:

The required result is to allow only Steve access to any SCSI devices.

The first optional result is to allow only John access to the Zip drive.

The second optional result is to allow only John access to the multiple video display capability of Windows 98.

The proposed solution is to create a hardware profile for John that disables the SCSI devices and Zip drive and use the original configuration hardware profile for Steve.

What does the proposed solution provide?

A. The required result and both of the optional results.

B. The required result and one of the optional results.

C. The required result but none of the optional results.

D. The proposed solution does not produce the required result.

70-098.03.06.001

Steve and John share a Windows 98 computer. The computer has the following components installed in it: a sound card, three video cards, a modem, a parallel Zip drive, a SCSI controller with a hard drive and CD-ROM, and a parallel CD-ROM and disk drive. When setting up the computer, you need the following results:

The required result is to allow only Steve access to any SCSI devices.

The first optional result is to allow only John access to the Zip drive.

The second optional result is to allow only John access to the multiple video display capability of Windows 98.

The proposed solution is to create a hardware profile for John that disables the SCSI devices and Zip drive and use the original configuration hardware profile for Steve.

What does the proposed solution provide?

► **Correct Answer: C**

  A. **Incorrect.** By using the original hardware profile, Steve will have access to the Zip drive and multiple display support. Therefore, neither optional result will be achieved.

  B. **Incorrect.** Neither optional result will be obtained since the original hardware profile will allow Steve to access the Zip drive. In addition, by disabling the Zip drive in John's profile, he will not have access to the device.

  C. **Correct.** Only the required result will be achieved. John will not have access to the Zip drive. Further, by using the original hardware profile for Steve, John will not have exclusive access to certain devices.

  D. **Incorrect.** The required result will be achieved but none of the optional results will be accomplished. A separate hardware profile, rather than the original, will have to be implemented to realize any of the optional results.

70-098.03.06.002

Steve and John share a Windows 98 computer. The computer has the following components installed in it: a sound card, three video cards, a modem, a parallel Zip drive, a SCSI controller with a hard drive and CD-ROM, and a parallel CD-ROM and disk drive. When setting up the computer, you need the following results:

The required result is to allow only Steve access to any SCSI devices.

The first optional result is to allow only John access to the Zip drive.

The second optional result is to allow only John access to the multiple video display capability of Windows 98.

The proposed solution is to create a hardware profile for Steve which disables the Zip drive and use the original configuration hardware profile for John.

What does the proposed solution provide?

A. The required result and both of the optional results.

B. The required result and one of the optional results.

C. The required result but none of the optional results.

D. The proposed solution does not produce the required result.

70-098.03.06.002

Steve and John share a Windows 98 computer. The computer has the following components installed in it: a sound card, three video cards, a modem, a parallel Zip drive, a SCSI controller with a hard drive and CD-ROM, and a parallel CD-ROM and disk drive. When setting up the computer, you need the following results:

The required result is to allow only Steve access to any SCSI devices.

The first optional result is to allow only John access to the Zip drive.

The second optional result is to allow only John access to the multiple video display capability of Windows 98.

The proposed solution is to create a hardware profile for Steve which disables the Zip drive and use the original configuration hardware profile for John.

What does the proposed solution provide?

▶ **Correct Answer: D**

A. **Incorrect.** The required result is not achieved since the original profile will allow John access to the SCSI devices. In addition, the custom profile for Steve does not restrict his access to devices. Therefore, neither optional results will be achieved.

B. **Incorrect.** The required result is not achieved since the original profile will allow John access to the SCSI devices. In addition, the custom profile for Steve does not restrict his access to devices. Therefore, neither optional results will be achieved.

C. **Incorrect.** The required result is not achieved since the original profile will allow John access to the SCSI devices.

D. **Correct.** By restricting Steve's access to the Zip drive, the required result of giving Steve exclusive access to the SCSI devices will not be achieved.

70-098.03.06.003

Steve and John share a Windows 98 computer. The computer has the following components installed in it: a sound card, three video cards, a modem, a parallel Zip drive, a SCSI controller with a hard drive and CD-ROM, and a parallel CD-ROM and disk drive. When setting up the computer, you need the following results:

The required result is to allow only Steve access to any SCSI devices.

The first optional result is to allow only John access to the Zip drive.

The second optional result is to allow only John access to the multiple video display capability of Windows 98.

The proposed solution is to create a hardware profile for Steve that disables the Zip drive and create a hardware profile for John which disables the SCSI devices and two of the video cards.

What does the proposed solution provide?

A. The required result and both of the optional results.

B. The required result and one of the optional results.

C. The required result but none of the optional results.

D. The proposed solution does not produce the required result.

70-098.03.06.003

Steve and John share a Windows 98 computer. The computer has the following components installed in it: a sound card, three video cards, a modem, a parallel Zip drive, a SCSI controller with a hard drive and CD-ROM, and a parallel CD-ROM and disk drive. When setting up the computer, you need the following results:

The required result is to allow only Steve access to any SCSI devices.

The first optional result is to allow only John access to the Zip drive.

The second optional result is to allow only John access to the multiple video display capability of Windows 98.

The proposed solution is to create a hardware profile for Steve that disables the Zip drive and create a hardware profile for John which disables the SCSI devices and two of the video cards.

What does the proposed solution provide?

▶ **Correct Answer: B**

    A. **Incorrect.** By disabling video card access for John, he will not have exclusive access to the multiple display support. Therefore, only one of the optional results will be achieved.

    B. **Correct.** The required result will be achieved by implementing the custom profiles. Further, by disabling Steve's access to the Zip drive, the first optional result will be achieved.

    C. **Incorrect.** By disabling Steve's access to the Zip drive, the first optional result will be achieved.

    D. **Incorrect.** By disabling SCSI access in John's profile, Steve will have exclusive access to these devices. Therefore, the required result will be achieved.

70-098.03.06.004

A user has a laptop. He uses it in a "docked" state half of the time but in an "undocked" state the rest of the time. What does the user need to do to configure the different hardware profiles?

A. Create a hardware profile to use when the computer is docked.

B. Create a hardware profile to use when the computer is undocked.

C. Nothing, Windows 98 automatically configures the computer correctly.

D. Create a hardware profile to use both when the computer is docked and undocked.

70-098.03.06.004

A user has a laptop. He uses it in a "docked" state half of the time but in an "undocked" state the rest of the time. What does the user need to do to configure the different hardware profiles?

▶ **Correct Answer: C**

A. **Incorrect.** Windows 98 can autodetect a docked or undocked state for laptops. Therefore, appropriate hardware profiles are automatically configured by Windows 98. You do not have to create a "docked" hardware profile.

B. **Incorrect.** Windows 98 can autodetect a docked or undocked state for laptops. Therefore, appropriate hardware profiles are automatically configured by Windows 98. You do not have to create an "undocked" hardware profile.

C. **Correct.** Since Windows 98 can autodetect a docked state, you do not have to manually create separate hardware profiles. These profiles will be created automatically by Windows 98.

D. **Incorrect.** Windows 98 can autodetect a docked or undocked state for laptops. Therefore, appropriate hardware profiles are automatically configured by Windows 98. You do not have to manually create different hardware profiles.

Further Reading

Microsoft Windows 98 Training Kit. Complete Lesson 1, "Configuring Hardware Settings," of Chapter 6, "Configuring Windows 98." In this lesson, implementing hardware profiles using Control Panel is discussed.

Windows 98 Accelerated MCSE Study Guide. Read Chapter 6, "Hardware Configuration," to learn more about implementing custom hardware profiles.

Integration and Interoperability

Depending on the type of network you will connect to, Windows 98 supports both Microsoft networks using Windows NT and Novell networks using NetWare. In addition to local networks, Windows 98 can access remote networks using dial-up technologies provided through modems or ISDN devices. For accessing external networks, such as the public Internet, Microsoft Windows 98 includes the Internet Explorer Web browser. Internet Explorer includes features to block potentially harmful content from being downloaded onto the local system. Internet Explorer also allows users to connect to the Internet via a proxy server. In addition, support is included for "kiosk mode," which can be used to allow public access to the Internet.

You will need a good understanding of the various capabilities to connect a Windows 98 client to a network. Implementing file and printer sharing for both network types is required. In addition, you will need to know how to configure Dial-Up Networking to create dial-up connections.

Tested Skills and Suggested Practices

The skills you need to successfully master the Integration and Interoperability Objective Domain on the exam include:

- **Accessing a Microsoft Windows NT network.**

  - Practice 1: Using the Network Neighborhood properties sheet, install Client for Microsoft Networks. Connect to a Windows NT Server resource to test the configuration.

  - Practice 2: Install and configure Dial-Up Networking and dial in to a Windows NT server.

  - Practice 3: Using an established dial-up connection to a Windows NT Server computer, connect to and use a file share and a shared printer.

- **Accessing a Novell NetWare network.**

  - Practice 1: Using the Network Neighborhood properties sheet, install Client for NetWare Networks. Connect to a NetWare server resource to test the configuration.

- **Installing a network protocol.**

  - Practice 1: From the Network Neighborhood properties sheet, manually add the TCP/IP protocol.

  - Practice 2: Without any support for Novell networks, install support for NetWare Directory Services. Notice the other NetWare-based components that are installed (Client for NetWare Networks and IPX/SPX).

- **Securing Windows 98 for Internet use.**

  - Practice 1: Configure Internet Explorer to access only sites that are not listed in the Restricted Sites zone.

  - Practice 2: Configure Internet Explorer for use with a proxy server.

OBJECTIVE 4.1

Configure a Windows 98 computer as a client computer in a Windows NT network.

There are generally two categories of networks that a Windows 98 client will connect to: a local network accessed via a network card and a remote network accessed via a modem or ISDN device. Local networks will require either Client for Microsoft Networks or Client for NetWare Networks. In the case of a remote network, you will need to install and configure an additional network component called Dial-Up Networking.

This objective covers accessing both Microsoft and Novell networks using Windows 98. In addition, you will also need to know how to configure Dial-Up Networking for use via a modem or ISDN device. Various protocols are covered, and you will need to know the default protocols when using a Microsoft (NetBEUI), NetWare (IPX/SPX), or remote (PPP) network. You'll also need to know when to use other protocols based on the network environment, such as TCP/IP.

To successfully answer the questions for this objective, you need a firm understanding of several key terms. For definitions of these terms, refer to the Glossary in this book.

Key Terms

- IP address

- NetBEUI

- Network protocol

- Peer-to-peer network

- Point-to-Point Protocol (PPP)

- Point-to-Point Tunneling Protocol (PPTP)

- Transmission Control Protocol/Internet Protocol (TCP/IP)

70-098.04.01.001

Which components are required for a Windows 98 computer to access resources on a Microsoft network? (Choose two.)

A. TCP/IP

B. Client for Microsoft Networks

C. A networking protocol in common

D. File and Printer Sharing for NetWare Networks

E. File and Printer Sharing for Microsoft Networks

70-098.04.01.002

You want to install a single protocol on your peer-to-peer network. Which protocol is recommended for a nine-node workgroup that consists of all Windows 98 computers?

A. DLC

B. TCP/IP

C. IPX/SPX

D. NetBEUI

70-098.04.01.001

Which components are required for a Windows 98 computer to access resources on a Microsoft network? (Choose two.)

▶ **Correct Answers: B and C**

  A. **Incorrect.** TCP/IP alone will not allow a Windows 98 computer access to resources that have been shared on a Windows NT network. You must also include Client for Microsoft Networks. Moreover, if TCP/IP is only installed on the Windows 98 computer, it will not allow access to rescources.

  B. **Correct.** Client for Microsoft Networks is one of the two network components that must be installed.

  C. **Correct.** For any two computers to connect with one another, they must both be running a common protocol.

  D. **Incorrect.** File and Printer Sharing for either Microsoft Networks or NetWare Networks is not required to access another computer's resources. File and printer sharing is required only if the Windows 98 computer plans to share its own resources.

  E. **Incorrect.** File and Printer Sharing for either Microsoft Networks or NetWare Networks is not required to access another computer's resources. File and printer sharing is required only if the Windows 98 computer plans to share its own resources.

70-098.04.01.002

You want to install a single protocol on your peer-to-peer network. Which protocol is recommended for a nine-node workgroup that consists of all Windows 98 computers?

▶ **Correct Answer: D**

  A. **Incorrect.** DLC is used to connect to network printers or an AS/400. Using DLC will not allow Windows 98 systems to access one another's resources.

  B. **Incorrect.** TCP/IP is commonly used to access computers across the public Internet. However, TCP/IP is not the most efficient protocol in a local area network environment that does not require routing.

  C. **Incorrect.** The IPX/SPX protocol is used to connect clients and servers on a Novell network, not a Microsoft network.

  D. **Correct.** NetBEUI is the best protocol in this environment because it requires the least amount of overhead and is easiest to maintain.

70-098.04.01.003

You have your TCP/IP settings set to automatically obtain an IP address. What happens if your DHCP server is not found to assign you an IP address?

A. You will not be able to log on to the network.

B. The computer will assign itself an address of 254.169.x.x.

C. The computer will assign itself an address of 169.254.x.x.

D. The TCP/IP configuration screen appears so you can input a valid address.

70-098.04.01.004

Examine the network adapter binding order shown below.

Your network has recently changed from the NetBEUI protocol to TCP/IP. You have noticed slower network performance.

How can you improve the access speed?

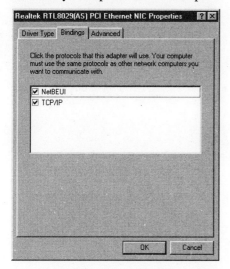

A. Add the IPX/SPX protocol.

B. Make NetBEUI the last bound protocol.

C. Make TCP/IP the first bound protocol.

D. Disable the NetBEUI protocol from the network card.

70-098.04.01.003

You have your TCP/IP settings set to automatically obtain an IP address. What happens if your DHCP server is not found to assign you an IP address?

▶ **Correct Answer: C**

    A. **Incorrect.** Windows 98 will automatically assign itself an IP address so you can access resources on the network. However, those resources must also be configured with an automatic IP address. The IP address will remain in use until a DHCP server is found.

    B. **Incorrect.** The computer will assign itself an IP address in the 169.254.x.x range. The IP address will remain in use until a DHCP server is found.

    C. **Correct.** Windows 98 will automatically assign itself an IP address via Automatic Private IP Addressing. This range is 169.254.x.x. The IP address will remain in use until a DHCP server is found.

    D. **Incorrect.** The TCP/IP window will not appear. Instead Windows 98 will automatically configure itself with an address in the 169.254.x.x range. The IP address will remain in use until a DHCP server is found.

70-098.04.01.004

Examine the network adapter binding order shown on the previous page.

Your network has recently changed from the NetBEUI protocol to TCP/IP. You have noticed slower network performance.

▶ **Correct Answer: D**

    A. **Incorrect.** Adding the IPX/SPX protocol will not increase network performance. Adding an additional protocol may slow the network even further. Consider removing the used NetBEUI protocol.

    B. **Incorrect.** Having more than one protocol installed can slow down network performance. If NetBEUI is no longer required, it should be removed.

    C. **Incorrect.** The order of binding will not necessarily increase network performance. Consider removing the used NetBEUI protocol.

    D. **Correct.** Only by removing unused protocols can you increase network performance.

70-098.04.01.005

What is the default Dial-Up Networking protocol?

A. PPP

B. PPTP

C. SLIP

D. CSLIP

E. TCP/IP

70-098.04.01.005

What is the default Dial-Up Networking protocol?

▶ **Correct Answer: A**

A. **Correct.** Dial-Up Networking uses Point-to-Point Protocol (PPP) by default.

B. **Incorrect.** Dial-Up Networking does not use Point-to-Point Tunneling Protocol (PPTP).

C. **Incorrect.** Dial-Up Networking does not support Serial Line Internet Protocol (SLIP) and therefore does not use it as the default protocol. SLIP is a viable connection protocol for Dial-Up Networking with Windows 98. The only restriction is that with Windows 98 there are no SLIP server capabilities, only dial-out client capabilities.

D. **Incorrect.** Dial-Up Networking does not support Compressed Serial Line Internet Protocol (CSLIP).

E. **Incorrect.** While Dial-Up Networking supports TCP/IP, it does not use it by default. It is not a connection protocol like PPP or SLIP. It cannot be selected to access a remote network through Dial-Up Networking.

70-098.04.01.006

A sales representative for your company works 50 percent of the time at your corporate office in New York and 50 percent of the time in the Ukraine.

The required result is to give the sales representative access to your network every day for short periods.

The first optional result is to avoid incurring long distance telephone charges when establishing the connection.

The second optional result is to provide a very secure connection.

The proposed solution is to implement a virtual private network using the PPTP protocol.

What does the proposed solution provide?

A. The required result and all optional results.

B. The required result and one optional result.

C. The required result but none of the optional results.

D. The proposed solution does not provide the required result.

70-098.04.01.006

A sales representative for your company works 50 percent of the time at your corporate office in New York and 50 percent of the time in the Ukraine.

The required result is to give the sales representative access to your network every day for short periods.

The first optional result is to avoid incurring long distance telephone charges when establishing the connection.

The second optional result is to provide a very secure connection.

The proposed solution is to implement a virtual private network using the PPTP protocol.

What does the proposed solution provide?

▶ **Correct Answer: A**

A. **Correct.** Using PPTP solves all requirements since the connection can be made when convenient, can be made via the Internet to reduce costs, and is highly encrypted for security.

B. **Incorrect.** All results will be achieved since the connection will be made over the Internet and it will be encrypted.

C. **Incorrect.** Both optimal results will be achieved since the connection will be made over the Internet and it will be encrypted.

D. **Incorrect.** The required result will be achieved since the users can access the network at their convenience via the Internet.

70-098.04.01.007

A sales representative for your company works 50 percent of the time at your corporate office in New York and 50 percent of the time in the Ukraine.

The required result is to give the sales representative access to your network every day for short periods.

The first optional result is to avoid incurring long distance telephone charges when establishing the connection.

The second optional result is to provide a very secure connection.

The proposed solution is to implement a Dial-Up Networking connection using the PPP protocol.

What does the proposed solution provide?

A. The required result and all optional results.

B. The required result and one optional result.

C. The required result but none of the optional results.

D. The proposed solution does not provide the required result.

70-098.04.01.007

A sales representative for your company works 50 percent of the time at your corporate office in New York and 50 percent of the time in the Ukraine.

The required result is to give the sales representative access to your network every day for short periods.

The first optional result is to avoid incurring long distance telephone charges when establishing the connection.

The second optional result is to provide a very secure connection.

The proposed solution is to implement a Dial-Up Networking connection using the PPP protocol.

What does the proposed solution provide?

▶ **Correct Answer: C**

A. **Incorrect.** Dialing into the local network from a long distance location is not the most cost-effective solution. Consider using an Internet-based virtual connection.

B. **Incorrect.** Neither optional result will be realized. PPP is not the most secure protocol available, and dialing directly into the corporate network is not the most cost-effective solution. Consider using PPTP as the protocol and using an Internet-based virtual network connection to reduce costs.

C. **Correct.** Only the required result will be realized. Both security and costs remain considerations for improvement.

D. **Incorrect.** Providing a dial-up connection directly into the corporate network will provide the user access to the network. However, this is not the most secure nor the most cost-effective solution.

Further Reading

Microsoft Windows 98 Training Kit. Complete Lesson 3, "Using Windows NT Network Resources," of Chapter 13, "Using Windows 98 on a Windows NT Network." In this lesson you will learn how to use user-level security and assign permission to shared folders on a per-user basis.

Microsoft Windows 98 Resource Kit. Read pages 601–602 to learn more about Automatic Private IP Addressing.

Windows 98 Accelerated MCSE Study Guide. Read Chapter 11, "Remote Connections," to learn more about the dial-up connection features of Windows 98.

OBJECTIVE 4.2

Configure a Windows 98 computer as a client computer in a NetWare network.

Windows 98 includes support for Novell NetWare networks. By installing the Client for NetWare Networks component, you can access printers and file shares on a NetWare server. The Windows 98 computer appears as a NetWare client. User-level security is the only security scheme available. Novell networks do not provide support for share-level security. While you can use the older NetWare 3.x client software (NETX), Windows 98's Client for NetWare Networks is more efficient.

You can also support NetWare Directory Services from Windows 98. To do this, you must install Microsoft Service for NetWare Directory Services. When you install this component, it will verify that the Internetwork Packet Exchange/Sequenced Packet Exchange (IPX/SPX) protocol and the Client for NetWare Networks are installed. If they are not, Microsoft Service for NetWare Directory Services will install them automatically.

To successfully answer the questions for this objective, you need a firm understanding of several key terms. For definitions of these terms, refer to the Glossary in this book.

Key Terms

- Internetwork Packet Exchange/Sequenced Packet Exchange (IPX/SPX)

- NetWare 3.x client software (NETX)

- NetWare Directory Services (NDS)

- Virtual Loadable Module (VLM)

70-098.04.02.001

Which networking client software can you use with Windows 98 to connect to NetWare 3.x or 4.x servers? (Choose all that apply.)

A. VLM

B. NETX

C. Novell Client for Windows 95/98

D. Novell Client for DOS/Windows 3.x

E. Microsoft Client for NetWare Networks

F. Microsoft Service for NetWare Directory Services

70-098.04.02.002

You are installing 10 Windows 98 computers on an existing NetWare 3.x network. Your client wants to use Novell's NETX client software. Which networking protocol should you use?

A. Microsoft's TCP/IP

B. Novell's NetWare /IP

C. Novell's real-mode IPX

D. Microsoft's 32-bit IPX/SPX

70-098.04.02.001

Which networking client software can you use with Windows 98 to connect to NetWare 3.x or 4.x servers? (Choose all that apply.)

▶ **Correct Answers: A, B, C, and E**

    A. **Correct.** Windows 98 supports the Novell VLM application.

    B. **Correct.** Windows 98 will supports the Novell NETX application. However, Microsoft Client for NetWare Networks is recommended instead of the older NETX.

    C. **Correct.** Windows 98 does support the Novell client for Windows 95, although the Microsoft Client for NetWare Networks component is recommended instead.

    D. **Incorrect.** The older Novell clients are not supported under Windows 98.

    E. **Correct.** Client for NetWare Networks is the recommended client software when connecting to a Novell network.

    F. **Incorrect.** Do not use Microsoft Service for NetWare Directory Services to connect to NetWare servers. Instead, use the Microsoft Client for NetWare Networks component.

70-098.04.02.002

You are installing 10 Windows 98 computers on an existing NetWare 3.x network. Your client wants to use Novell's NETX client software. Which networking protocol should you use?

▶ **Correct Answer: C**

    A. **Incorrect.** When connecting to a Novell network, you need to use a version of the IPX/SPX protocol.

    B. **Incorrect.** Novell's NetWare/IP is an IP routable protocol that is not as efficient as IPX on a local area network that uses NetWare servers.

    C. **Correct.** NETX is optimized to use Novell's real-mode IPX instead of the 32-bit IPX/SPX protocol provided by Microsoft.

    D. **Incorrect.** Microsoft's 32-bit IPX/SPX is not optimized for use with NETX. If you want to use the 32-bit IPX/SPX, you will need to use Client for NetWare Networks instead of NETX.

70-098.04.02.003

You are installing 30 Windows 98 workstations on your NetWare 4.x network, which uses NetWare Directory Services (NDS). In one step, you want to install all necessary networking components on the workstation. Which component must you install?

A. TCP/IP

B. IPX/SPX

C. Client for NetWare Networks

D. File and Printer Sharing for NetWare Networks

E. Microsoft Service for NetWare Directory Services

70-098.04.02.004

What must be installed on a Windows 98 computer for it to connect to with a NetWare 4.x server? (Choose all that apply.)

A. Novell Open Data-Link Interface (ODI) IPX protocol

B. Client for NetWare Networks

C. IPX/SPX-compatible protocol

D. Service for NetWare Directory Service

E. File and Printer Sharing for NetWare Networks

70-098.04.02.003

You are installing 30 Windows 98 workstations on your NetWare 4.x network, which uses NetWare Directory Services (NDS). In one step, you want to install all necessary networking components on the workstation. Which component must you install?

▶ **Correct Answer: E**

A. **Incorrect.** TCP/IP does not provide Windows 98 clients access to a Novell network. Only if you install Microsoft Service for NetWare Directory Services will all the required components be installed.

B. **Incorrect.** IPX/SPX alone will not provide access to the Novell resources. If you install Microsoft Service for NetWare Directory Services, all the required components will be installed.

C. **Incorrect.** Client for NetWare Networks will automatically install IPX/SPX and Microsoft Service for NetWare Directory Services.

D. **Incorrect.** File and Printer Sharing for NetWare Networks will not install all the required components.

E. **Correct.** Only if you install Microsoft Service for NetWare Directory Services will all the other Novell components be installed automatically. However, each individual component can be installed manually if you prefer.

70-098.04.02.004

What must be installed on a Windows 98 computer for it to connect to with a NetWare 4.x server? (Choose all that apply.)

▶ **Correct Answers: B and C**

A. **Incorrect.** Novell's IPX is not suggested, or required, to access a NetWare network from Windows 98. Consider installing Microsoft's 32-bit IPX/SPX and Client for NetWare Networks.

B. **Correct.** Client for NetWare Networks is required to access Novell resources.

C. **Correct.** IPX/SPX is the protocol used by Novell network operating systems and is therefore required.

D. **Incorrect.** NDS is not required by Windows 98 to connect to a NetWare server resource.

E. **Incorrect.** File and Printer Sharing for NetWare Networks is only required to allow NetWare clients to access a Windows 98 shared resource. This component is not required to have a Windows 98 computer connect to a NetWare server.

Further Reading

Microsoft Windows 98 Training Kit. Complete Lesson 2, "Logging on to a NetWare Server," of Chapter 14, "Using Windows 98 on a Novell Network." In this lesson, configuring IPX/SPX and the NetWare network components is discussed.

Microsoft Windows 98 Resource Kit. Read pages 792–793 to learn more about File and Printer Sharing for NetWare Networks.

Windows 98 Accelerated MCSE Study Guide. Read Chapter 8, "Network Configuration," to learn more about accessing NetWare networks.

OBJECTIVE 4.3

Configure a Windows 98 computer for remote access.

Windows 98 can provide remote access by using various methods in a Microsoft environment and a mixed Microsoft and NetWare environment. Windows 98 can be configured to connect to a remote network using the Dial-Up Networking component. Either a modem or ISDN device can be used to dial in to the network. Once a connection has been made, both Client for Microsoft Networks and Client for NetWare Networks can then be used to access resources on the remote network.

The other remote access method covered by this objective is the use of a proxy server. Through Microsoft Internet Explorer, Windows 98 can be configured to access network resources via a proxy server. In addition, Internet Explorer can be configured to restrict access to Web sites that may potentially contain dangerous content. For organizations that want to use Windows 98 as a public Internet access point, Internet Explorer can be run in "kiosk mode." In kiosk mode, Windows 98 can act as a workstation to the Internet, such as on computers in a public library.

To successfully answer the questions for this objective, you need a firm understanding of several key terms. For definitions of these terms, refer to the Glossary in this book.

Key Terms

- Domain name

- Firewall

- Host name

- Network protocol

- Proxy server

- URL

70-098.04.03.001

You want to connect to your company's Windows NT domain using a modem. What will you need to install and/or configure on your Windows 98 computer? (Choose two.)

A. Log on to the network before connecting.

B. Configure your server type as a SLIP server.

C. Install File and Printer Sharing for Microsoft Networks.

D. Input the telephone number, username, and password for the RAS server.

E. Install a common networking protocol between the host and the user's computer.

70-098.04.03.002

A user on your Windows network needs to change his Internet Explorer's home page. How can this be configured?

A. Connect to http://home.microsoft.com and personalize your start page.

B. Add the URL of the Web site you want in your user profile from Internet Explorer's Internet Options.

C. Enter the URL of the Web site in the Address box of the General tab from Internet Explorer's Internet Options.

D. Enter the URL of the Web site you want in the Content Provider tab of Internet Options.

70-098.04.03.001

You want to connect to your company's Windows NT domain using a modem. What will you need to install and/or configure on your Windows 98 computer? (Choose two.)

▶ **Correct Answers: D and E**

   A. **Incorrect.** You cannot log on to the network until you have connected to the Windows NT server.

   B. **Incorrect.** PPP is the default Dial-Up Networking protocol and should be used over SLIP.

   C. **Incorrect.** You do not need to install File and Printer Sharing to connect to a Windows NT server via Dial-Up Networking.

   D. **Correct.** You must enter the phone number and user validation information before you can connect to a RAS server.

   E. **Correct.** You will always need a common protocol between two computers over any network, including dial-up networks.

70-098.04.03.002

A user on your Windows network needs to change his Internet Explorer's home page. How can this be configured?

▶ **Correct Answer: C**

   A. **Incorrect.** You can configure a startup page in the Internet Explorer's Internet Options menu. You do not need to connect to Microsoft's Web site.

   B. **Incorrect.** You add the URL to the Home Page item under Internet Options.

   C. **Correct.** Under View, Internet Options, you can specify a URL, have Internet Explorer use the current URL, specify the default, or set it to a blank page.

   D. **Incorrect.** You can specify a start page on the General tab, not the Content tab.

70-098.04.03.003

You want to prevent users from accessing Web sites on the Internet that could be potentially dangerous to their Windows 98 computer. Which security zone would most likely prevent this?

A. Internet zone

B. Trusted Sites zone

C. Local Intranet zone

D. Restricted Sites zone

70-098.04.03.004

How can computers that obtain their IP address from Automatic Private IP Addressing access the Internet? (Choose two.)

A. Use RAS.

B. Use a proxy server.

C. Wait until their DHCP server comes back online.

D. Use a Network Address Translation (NAT) gateway.

E. They cannot access the Internet with Automatic Private IP Addressing.

70-098.04.03.003

You want to prevent users from accessing Web sites on the Internet that could be potentially dangerous to their Windows 98 computer. Which security zone would most likely prevent this?

▶ **Correct Answer: D**

A. **Incorrect.** Internet zone is the most open and nonsecure zone and would expose users to potentially dangerous content.

B. **Incorrect.** While trusted sites are a bit more secure than the Internet zone, users could still access potentially dangerous content.

C. **Incorrect.** The Local Intranet zone is very secure, but still does not provide the highest level of security.

D. **Correct.** Only the Restricted Sites zone will ensure that those sites that could cause harm will not be accessed.

70-098.04.03.004

How can computers that obtain their IP address from Automatic Private IP Addressing access the Internet? (Choose two.)

▶ **Correct Answers: B and D**

A. **Incorrect.** The Remote Access Server will not provide automatic IP addressing and therefore is not one of the possible solutions.

B. **Correct.** A proxy server would provide the user access to the Internet until a valid IP address is issued.

C. **Incorrect.** Once a DHCP server comes online, the IP address provided will be replaced. Therefore, this solution is not correct based on the requirements of the question.

D. **Correct.** A NAT gateway is the only way, other than using a proxy server, that these users could access the Internet.

E. **Incorrect.** Using either a proxy server or a NAT gateway, systems that have an automatic IP address assigned can connect to the Internet.

70-098.04.03.005

What is the host name of the URL address http://www.microsoft.com/default.asp?

A. www

B. com

C. http

D. microsoft

E. www.microsoft.com

70-098.04.03.006

Which method of regulating Web traffic can examine and filter all packets based on parameters set by an administrative policy?

A. Firewall

B. Proxy server

C. RSAC ratings

D. Security settings

70-098.04.03.005

What is the host name of the URL address http://www.microsoft.com/default.asp?

▶ **Correct Answer: A**

A. **Correct.** The name to the left of the domain is the host name; in this case, "www".

B. **Incorrect.** "com" is not the host name; it is the domain type.

C. **Incorrect.** HTTP specifies the protocol, not the host name.

D. **Incorrect.** This is the domain name, not the individual computer being connected to. In this case, the machine configured as "www" is the host.

E. **Incorrect.** "www.microsoft.com" is the complete name of the computer being connected to, not just the host name.

70-098.04.03.006

Which method of regulating Web traffic can examine and filter all packets based on parameters set by an administrative policy?

▶ **Correct Answer: A**

A. **Correct.** Only a firewall can filter unwanted packets based on the requirements defined by the system administrator. This provides for a high level of security in allowing only approved access into and out of the network.

B. **Incorrect.** Proxy servers are used to control access out of the network. A firewall is used to control access into the network. Often the terms proxy and firewall are used interchangeably, but they do, in fact, provide different capabilities.

C. **Incorrect.** Recreational Software Advisory Council (RSAC) does not control what packets are filtered on a network.

D. **Incorrect.** Security settings control individual or computer access. To manage access at a packet level, you need to implement a firewall.

Further Reading

Microsoft Windows 98 Training Kit. Complete Lesson 2, "Controlling Access to Internet Content," of Chapter 17, "Using Windows 98 and the Internet." In this lesson, you will learn how to secure the Internet Explorer and use a proxy server to access content on the Internet.

Microsoft Windows 98 Training Kit. Complete Lesson 1, "Setting Up Dial-Up Networking," of Chapter 18, "Implementing Dial-Up Networking in Windows 98." In this lesson, configuring Dial-Up Networking and the necessary hardware components, such as a modem or ISDN device, will be discussed.

Monitoring and Optimization

Although this objective domain contains only two objectives, it covers a large variety of troubleshooting and maintenance tools. For the exam, you will be required to understand how to apply these tools to help you monitor and optimize your Windows 98 configuration. There are three main categories with which you need to be familiar:

- Obtaining current system information
- Backing up and restoring the system registry
- Managing compressed file systems

The Microsoft System Information utility can help you determine the current state of the system. Both registry maintenance tools, the Windows Registry Checker and Microsoft Registry Checker, are used to manage the registry. Using DriveSpace3, you can compress and manage drives. Overall, you will need a good understanding of what tools are available and the services they provide.

Tested Skills and Suggested Practices

The skills you need to successfully master the Monitoring and Optimization Objective Domain on the exam include:

- **Checking the state of the system.**

    - Practice 1: Use the Microsoft System Information utility (MSInfo) to gather current information about the computer.

    - Practice 2: Start the System Monitor and watch system activity in a "real-time" state.

- **Managing disk drives.**

  - Practice 1: Run ScanDisk to check a local hard drive.

  - Practice 2: Start Disk Defragmenter to defrag a local drive.

- **Managing compressed drives.**

  - Practice 1: Install Windows 98 using a FAT16 file system. Use the Compression Agent to compress individual files or an entire drive.

OBJECTIVE 5.1

Monitor system performance.

Windows 98 includes a number of tools to help you diagnose problems and check overall system performance. The Microsoft System Information utility is a centralized troubleshooting tool. You can use the System Information utility to view information about the computer's configuration. It also gives you a way to access several other Windows utilities, including the Windows Report Tool, Dr. Watson, and Scan-Disk. You can also save and export System Utility information.

In addition, you can use the Net Watcher utility to manage connected users and shared folders. Net Watcher requires Client for Microsoft Networks to be installed first. Using this tool, you can also manage remote computers in a peer-to-peer environment if the system supports remote administration.

For monitoring system performance, the Resource Meter utility provides live information about the current state of the Windows 98 computer. Resource Meter reports on overall system resources, user resources, and GDI resources. This is useful for a quick look at how the system is allocating its available resources.

To successfully answer the questions for this objective, you need a firm understanding of several key terms. For definitions of these terms, refer to the Glossary in this book.

Key Terms

- Automatic Skip Driver Agent

- Dr. Watson

- Net Watcher

- Resource Meter

- System Monitor

- Windows Registry Checker

- Windows Report Tool

70-098.05.01.001

A computer running Windows 98 in your office has become sluggish and less responsive over the last month. Before committing any resources to a major configuration change, you would like to evaluate the performance of the computer's memory, disks, and networking components. You need to keep a log of the results.

Which utility could you use to perform this task?

A. System Monitor

B. Device Manager

C. Microsoft System Information (MSInfo)

D. Microsoft Management Console

70-098.05.01.002

Which object should be monitored if you suspect you have a memory leak?

A. Swapfile

B. Kernel: Threads

C. Kernel: Processor Usage (%)

D. Memory Manager: Locked Memory

70-098.05.01.001

A computer running Windows 98 in your office has become sluggish and less responsive over the last month. Before committing any resources to a major configuration change, you would like to evaluate the performance of the computer's memory, disks, and networking components. You need to keep a log of the results.

Which utility could you use to perform this task?

▶ **Correct Answer: A**

A. **Correct.** System Monitor is the best tool to evaluate the overall aspects of Windows 98. You can chart activity and create a log for later review.

B. **Incorrect.** The Device Manager will only tell you whether all the hardware devices are configured properly.

C. **Incorrect.** The Microsoft System Information utility will not provide real-time performance information. Consider using the System Monitor to evaluate the computer's resources.

D. **Incorrect.** Microsoft Management Console is used to manage services such as Internet Information Server or Microsoft Transaction Server. It will not help evaluate the state of a Windows 98 computer.

70-098.05.01.002

Which object should be monitored if you suspect you have a memory leak?

▶ **Correct Answer: B**

A. **Incorrect.** The swapfile will not return information about a possible memory leak. Use the Kernel: Threads object instead.

B. **Correct.** Kernel: Threads will show if threads are being started by an application and not being reclaimed. When Windows 98 closes an application, it also closes these threads. So, for an application that has a memory leak, stopping and restarting the application will provide a temporary solution.

C. **Incorrect.** The Kernel: Processor Usage (%) will show which applications are using the processor, not return information about a possible memory leak.

D. **Incorrect.** Memory Manager: Locked Memory will show how much memory has been allocated. However, this will not be useful as an indicator to determine if a memory leak exists.

70-098.05.01.003

While using System Monitor, you notice an extremely high value for Memory Manager: Page Faults. Which actions would reduce the system load and decrease the page faults? (Choose two.)

A. Add RAM to the computer.

B. Close unused applications.

C. Increase the size of the swapfile.

D. Move the swapfile to a different disk partition.

70-098.05.01.004

Which Windows 98 tools can be accessed through the Tools menu of Microsoft System Information? (Choose all that apply.)

A. Dr. Watson

B. Registry Editor

C. Registry Checker

D. Performance Monitor

E. Windows Report Tool

F. Automatic Skip Driver Agent

70-098.05.01.003

While using System Monitor, you notice an extremely high value for Memory Manager: Page Faults. Which actions would reduce the system load and decrease the page faults? (Choose two.)

▶ **Correct Answers: A and B**

A. **Correct.** Page faults occur when there is not enough physical RAM on the system.

B. **Correct.** Since page faults occur as a result of not enough RAM, closing unnecessary applications will help reduce the number of times Windows 98 uses the swapfile.

C. **Incorrect.** Increasing the swapfile will not reduce page faults since a page fault occurs as a direct result of not enough physical RAM.

D. **Incorrect.** Moving the swapfile will have no effect on the number of page faults. Only reducing the amount of required RAM or increasing the amount of available RAM will solve this problem.

70-098.05.01.004

Which Windows 98 tools can be accessed through the Tools menu of Microsoft System Information? (Choose all that apply.)

▶ **Correct Answers: A, C, E, and F**

A. **Correct.** MSInfo will allow a number of troubleshooting tools to be launched from a convenient interface; Dr. Watson is one of them.

B. **Incorrect.** While MSInfo will launch a number of troubleshooting tools, the Registry Editor is not one of them. The Registry Editor should be used only in the event an interface does not already exist for making changes and should then be used very carefully.

C. **Correct.** MSInfo will allow a number of troubleshooting tools to be launched from a convenient interface; Registry Checker is one of them.

D. **Incorrect.** Performance Monitor is a Windows NT utility and is not supported by Windows 98.

E. **Correct.** MSInfo will allow a number of troubleshooting tools to be launched from a convenient interface; Windows Report Tool is one of them.

F. **Correct.** MSInfo will allow a number of troubleshooting tools to be launched from a convenient interface; Automatic Skip Driver Agent is one of them.

70-098.05.01.005

You need to view any failures to load or initialize drivers. Which Windows 98 file or tool allows you to monitor these procedures?

A. SCANREG

B. BOOTLOG.TXT

C. System Monitor

D. Maintenance Wizard

E. Performance Monitor

F. Microsoft System Information

70-098.05.01.005

You need to view any failures to load or initialize drivers. Which Windows 98 file or tool allows you to monitor these procedures?

▶ **Correct Answer: B**

   A. **Incorrect.** SCANREG is used to check the registry for errors and to back up the system registry. However, it is not used to evaluate which drivers have been loaded.

   B. **Correct.** BOOTLOG.TXT will provide information about the Windows 98 boot process that can be used to determine the status of various drivers.

   C. **Incorrect.** System Monitor will provide information about the system, but not the status of drivers that may have failed to load during the boot process.

   D. **Incorrect.** The Maintenance Wizard is used to schedule maintenance tasks. It does not provide information about which drivers haven't been loaded.

   E. **Incorrect.** Windows 98 does not support Performance Monitor.

   F. **Incorrect.** Microsoft System Information will provide data about the system, but not the status of drivers that may have failed to load during the boot process.

Further Reading

Microsoft Windows 98 Training Kit. Complete Lesson 1, "Viewing System Information," of Chapter 9, "Maintaining Windows 98 in a Stand-alone Environment." In this lesson you will learn how to use the Microsoft System Information utility to view details about the computer's configuration.

Microsoft Windows 98 Resource Kit. Read pages 1239–1243 to learn more about the Microsoft System Information utility (MSInfo).

Windows 98 Accelerated MCSE Study Guide. Read Chapter 15, "Tuning Windows 98," to learn more about the Net Watcher application.

O B J E C T I V E   5 . 2

Tune and optimize the system in a Microsoft environment and a mixed Microsoft and NetWare environment.

This objective includes a number of specific tasks that will be included on the exam. Each task has a utility associated with it to perform the tuning operation. When optimizing the hard disk, you can use both the Disk Defragmenter and ScanDisk tools. Disk Defragmenter includes an application optimization option that decreases the time it takes to start a program. Both the Windows-based and MS-DOS-based versions of ScanDisk have been upgraded to support both FAT16 and FAT32 file systems. In addition, the Disk Cleanup Wizard, a new tool in Windows 98, removes temporary and unneeded files.

When compressing files on a drive to increase available space, Windows 98 includes DriveSpace3 and the Compression Agent. Remember that FAT32 file systems cannot be compressed using the Compression Agent.

Windows 98 also provides Web-based resources that assist in accessing technical support and keeping the system up-to-date. Tools such as Windows Update, Windows Update Technical Support, can be used to maintain the latest versions of device drivers and system files. The Windows Report Tool can be used to send current status about a Windows 98 system to technical support personnel, such as those at a corporate help desk. The Version Conflict Manager is a utility that helps resolve potential system file (DLL) conflicts when upgrading a system to Windows 98.

Use the Maintenance Wizard as a quick and simple method for running ScanDisk, Disk Defragmenter, and Disk Cleanup unattended on a regular schedule. Using the Scheduled Tasks Wizard, you can schedule any application to run at a specific time.

Windows 98 provides two programs for backing up and restoring system configuration files, the Windows Registry Checker and the Microsoft Registry Checker. The Windows Registry Checker is a Windows-based program that scans and backs up the following files: USER.DAT, SYSTEM.DAT, WIN.INI, and SYSTEM.INI. The scan occurs automatically when the system is idle or when configuration changes are made. The Microsoft Registry Checker is an MS-DOS-based program that scans the system configuration files. If errors are found, the Microsoft Registry Checker restores a backup copy of the registry.

To successfully answer the questions for this objective, you need a firm understanding of several key terms. For definitions of these terms, refer to the Glossary in this book.

Key Terms

- Disk Defragmenter

- System Configuration Utility

- System File Checker

- Version Conflict Manager

- Windows Registry Checker

70-098.05.02.001

A user on your network upgraded to Windows 98 two months ago. He has noticed that applications no longer load as fast as they did when Windows 98 was first installed. Which action would improve software load times with the least amount of expense?

A. Run DEFRAG.

B. Install more RAM.

C. Upgrade to a faster processor.

D. Run ScanDisk with the automatic file repair option.

70-098.05.02.002

When does Registry Checker back up the registry?

A. Each time the computer is started.

B. When you log on to the computer.

C. Only the Windows Backup program can back up the registry.

D. Once each five system startups, or as configured in SCANREG.INI.

70-098.05.02.001

A user on your network upgraded to Windows 98 two months ago. He has noticed that applications no longer load as fast as they did when Windows 98 was first installed. Which action would improve software load times with the least amount of expense?

► **Correct Answer: A**

A. **Correct.** Over time, files can become fragmented on the hard drive. This can decrease performance. The DEFRAG utility will help increase system performance.

B. **Incorrect.** There is a less expensive option to solve this problem than installing more RAM. Consider using DEFRAG to optimize application startup.

C. **Incorrect.** There is a less expensive option to solve this problem than upgrading to a faster processor. Consider using DEFRAG to optimize application startup.

D. **Incorrect.** ScanDisk will repair problems with the file system. DEFRAG should be used to optimize how files are saved on the drive and increase application performance.

70-098.05.02.002

When does Registry Checker back up the registry?

► **Correct Answer: A**

A. **Correct.** The system registry is critical to Windows 98 providing a stable environment. Therefore, Registry Checker will automatically back up the registry each time the computer is started.

B. **Incorrect.** Registry Checker backs up the registry only when the system is started. You can, however, manually back up the registry.

C. **Incorrect.** The Registry Checker is the only tool that automatically backs up the registry when the computer is started.

D. **Incorrect.** The registry is backed up every time the system starts, not every five times.

70-098.05.02.003

Which files does the Windows Registry Checker back up? (Choose all that apply.)

A. WIN.INI

B. USER.INI

C. USER.DAT

D. SYSTEM.INI

E. SYSTEM.DAT

F. PROGMAN.INI

70-098.05.02.004

You would like to customize such features in Windows 98 as multiple boot configurations and initial startup delays. Which file should you edit to adjust these parameters?

A. IO.SYS

B. MSDOS.SYS

C. CONFIG.SYS

D. SYSTEM.INI

E. AUTOEXEC.BAT

70-098.05.02.003

Which files does the Windows Registry Checker back up? (Choose all that apply.)

▶ **Correct Answers: A, C, D, and E**

    A. **Correct.** WIN.INI is automatically included in the files that are saved when the registry is backed up.

    B. **Incorrect.** USER.INI is not included in the files automatically included in a registry backup.

    C. **Correct.** USER.DAT is automatically included in the files that are saved when the registry is backed up.

    D. **Correct.** SYSTEM.INI is automatically included in the files that are saved when the registry is backed up.

    E. **Correct.** SYSTEM.DAT is automatically included in the files that are saved when the registry is backed up.

    F. **Incorrect.** PROGMAN.INI is not included in the files automatically included in a registry backup.

70-098.05.02.004

You would like to customize such features in Windows 98 as multiple boot configurations and initial startup delays. Which file should you edit to adjust these parameters?

▶ **Correct Answer: B**

    A. **Incorrect.** While IO.SYS is a required file for starting your computer, it does not control bootup processes such as multiple configurations or startup delays.

    B. **Correct.** MSDOS.SYS provides a number of options for controlling the bootup process.

    C. **Incorrect.** CONFIG.SYS can be used to load drives, but does not control bootup processes like startup delays.

    D. **Incorrect.** SYSTEM.INI stores information about the Windows 98 system but does not allow you to configure settings such as startup delays.

    E. **Incorrect.** AUTOEXEC.BAT can be used to load applications before Windows 98 starts, but is not used for controlling bootup information such as multiple boot configurations.

70-098.05.02.005

Which Windows 98 utility has replaced the System Configuration Editor (Sysedit)?

A. MSDOS.SYS

B. Registry Editor

C. Registry Scanner

D. System Configuration Utility

70-098.05.02.006

A friend has edited your original SYSTEM.INI file and now an error occurs when you boot up the computer. You ran the System Configuration Utility before allowing your friend to work on the computer. After he leaves, you decide to restore the original file. What is the best way to restore the original SYSTEM.INI file?

A. Copy the SYSTEM.BAK file to SYSTEM.INI.

B. Restart the computer, press F5, and select Last Known Good Configuration.

C. Delete the current SYSTEM.INI file and restart the computer. The system will automatically restore a good SYSTEM.INI.

D. Use the System Configuration Utility and select the Restore Backup option. This will restore the previously saved *.PSS file.

70-098.05.02.005

Which Windows 98 utility has replaced the System Configuration Editor (Sysedit)?

▶ **Correct Answer: D**

A. **Incorrect.** MSDOS.SYS controls bootup processes. It was not designed to replace Sysedit.

B. **Incorrect.** The Registry Editor was not designed to replace Sysedit.

C. **Incorrect.** The Registry Scanner, SCANREG, was not designed to replace Sysedit.

D. **Correct.** System Configuration Utility (MSConfig) was designed to replace the older Sysedit application.

70-098.05.02.006

A friend has edited your original SYSTEM.INI file and now an error occurs when you boot up the computer. You ran the System Configuration Utility before allowing your friend to work on the computer. After he leaves, you decide to restore the original file. What is the best way to restore the original SYSTEM.INI file?

▶ **Correct Answer: D**

A. **Incorrect.** The backup is in a .PSS file and should only be restored using the System Configuration Utility.

B. **Incorrect.** Restarting the computer will not restore the previous SYSTEM.INI file.

C. **Incorrect.** You should never delete the SYSTEM.INI file. Use the System Configuration Utility to restore the previous version.

D. **Correct.** Only the System Configuration Utility can restore a previous SYSTEM.INI.

70-098.05.02.007

What must you do to view the properties of a hidden host drive with a DriveSpace3 Compressed Volume File (CVF) drive on it?

A. You cannot find information on a hidden host drive.

B. Run DriveSpace3, and view information on the drive.

C. Open a command prompt, log on to the drive, and run ScanDisk.

D. Open Windows Explorer, select the drive, and click Properties.

70-098.05.02.008

When you start Windows 98, you receive the following error message:

"Windows was unable to process the registry."

Which of the following actions will correct this error?

A. Copy the backup registry from the repair folder.

B. Restart the computer in safe mode and run ScanRegW.

C. Reboot to Command Prompt Only and run SCANREG /FIX.

D. Restart the computer. The Registry Scanner will perform an automatic repair.

70-098.05.02.007

What must you do to view the properties of a hidden host drive with a DriveSpace3 Compressed Volume File (CVF) drive on it?

▶ **Correct Answer: B**

A. **Incorrect.** Using DriveSpace3, you can view information about a hidden host drive.

B. **Correct.** DriveSpace3 allows you to view information about a hidden drive.

C. **Incorrect.** ScanDisk will not allow you to view information about a hidden drive.

D. **Incorrect.** You cannot view the properties of a hidden drive through Windows Explorer. Use the DriveSpace3 utility instead.

70-098.05.02.008

When you start Windows 98, you receive the following error message:

"Windows was unable to process the registry."

Which of the following actions will correct this error?

▶ **Correct Answer: C**

A. **Incorrect.** You should never attempt to edit or configure the registry manually. Use the SCANREG application to fix the registry.

B. **Incorrect.** The utility that should be used is called SCANREG and it should be launched from a command prompt, not safe mode.

C. **Correct.** If you run SCANREG with the /FIX parameter, the registry should be repaired, allowing you to log on to the system.

D. **Incorrect.** The registry will not automatically be fixed because Registry Scanner will not start by itself.

70-098.05.02.009

You receive an error message that a DLL file is missing or corrupt. Which tool would you use to replace it?

A. SCANREG

B. System File Checker

C. Maintenance Wizard

D. System Configuration Utility

70-098.05.02.010

Which performance-improving tasks can the Maintenance Wizard schedule? (Choose all that apply.)

A. SCANREG

B. ScanDisk

C. Disk Cleanup

D. Windows Update

E. Disk Defragmenter

F. Compression Agent

70-098.05.02.009

You receive an error message that a DLL file is missing or corrupt. Which tool would you use to replace it?

▶ **Correct Answer: B**

A. **Incorrect.** The Registry Scanner will only fix problems with the registry, not with system DLL files.

B. **Correct.** The System File Checker will reinstall missing or corrupt DLL files. You can also use this tool to back up system files before restoring the originals.

C. **Incorrect.** The Maintenance Wizard is used to schedule maintenance tasks, not restore DLL files.

D. **Incorrect.** The System Configuration Utility will provide information about the system and allow you to launch other troubleshooting tools. However, it cannot restore DLL files.

70-098.05.02.010

Which performance-improving tasks can the Maintenance Wizard schedule? (Choose all that apply.)

▶ **Correct Answers: B, C, E, and F**

A. **Incorrect.** To use the Registry Scanner, you must start it manually.

B. **Correct.** ScanDisk is a common maintenance task that the Maintenance Wizard can schedule.

C. **Correct.** Disk Cleanup is a task that can be scheduled by the Maintenance Wizard.

D. **Incorrect.** Windows Update must be run manually. It cannot be scheduled through the Maintenance Wizard.

E. **Correct.** Disk Defrag is a common maintenance task that the Maintenance Wizard can schedule.

F. **Correct.** The Compression Agent can be scheduled to run through the Maintenance Wizard.

70-098.05.02.011

You just upgraded your Windows 95 computer to Windows 98. When you start your Accounting application, you get an error message concerning missing DLL files. What is most likely causing this error and how can you correct the problem?

A. The installation of the program is nonrepairable and the program must be reinstalled.

B. Setup replaced the application's system files. Use the Version Conflict Manager to restore them.

C. The files that are missing are an older version. Contact the Accounting software vendor and obtain the newer files.

D. Setup renamed any system files that were not Windows 98–compatible. Restore the application's system files from a backup.

E. Setup renamed the system files with a *.DLT extension and copied them to C:\Windows\System. Locate the files, rename them, and copy them back to the C:\Windows directory.

70-098.05.02.011

You just upgraded your Windows 95 computer to Windows 98. When you start your Accounting application, you get an error message concerning missing DLL files. What is most likely causing this error and how can you correct the problem?

▶ **Correct Answer: B**

    A. **Incorrect.** It is possible that Windows 98 DLLs have caused a conflict. Try running the Version Conflict Manager before attempting to reinstall the application.

    B. **Correct.** The Version Conflict Manager can be used to diagnose problems that can occur when the Windows 98 Setup program overwrites an application's system DLLs during an upgrade from Windows 95. In addition, this utility can restore the original DLLs in order to fix applications that no longer function.

    C. **Incorrect.** You should run the Version Conflict Manager first to see if you can resolve the problem before contacting the vendor.

    D. **Incorrect.** You should not restore previous DLL files. Instead, run the Version Conflict Manager to resolve the problem.

    E. **Incorrect.** You should not restore previous DLL files. Instead, run the Version Conflict Manager to resolve the problem.

Further Reading

Microsoft Windows 98 Training Kit. Complete Lesson 4, "Automating Setup," of Chapter 2, "Installing Windows 98." In this lesson, you will learn about the use of setup scripts to help automate the installation of Windows 98 in a large environment.

Microsoft Windows 98 Training Kit. Complete Lesson 1, "Viewing System Information," of Chapter 9, "Maintaining Windows 98 in a Stand-alone Environment." In this lesson you will learn how to use the Microsoft System Information utility to view details about the computer's configuration.

Microsoft Windows 98 Training Kit. Complete Lesson 2, "Performing Maintenance Tasks," of Chapter 9, "Maintaining Windows 98 in a Stand-alone Environment." In this lesson you will learn how to use maintenance tools included with Windows 98. You will also learn how to use Scheduled Tasks to perform unattended maintenance.

Microsoft Windows 98 Training Kit. Complete Lesson 3, "Using Web-based Troubleshooting Tools," of Chapter 9, "Maintaining Windows 98 in a Stand-alone Environment." In this lesson the various Web-based update tools will be discussed.

Microsoft Windows 98 Training Kit. Complete Lesson 1, "Preparing for Troubleshooting," of Chapter 10, "Troubleshooting Windows 98 in a Stand-alone Environment." In this lesson you will learn how to use the Registry Checker to manually back up the registry, and you will learn how to create an Emergency Startup Disk.

Microsoft Windows 98 Resource Kit. Read pages 1258–1263 to learn more about the System Configuration Utility.

Microsoft Windows 98 Resource Kit. Read pages 1238–1239 to learn more about Windows 98 troubleshooting tools.

Microsoft Windows 98 Resource Kit. Read page 468 to learn about the File System Checker.

Windows 98 Accelerated MCSE Study Guide. Read Chapter 15, "Tuning Windows 98," to learn more about the various system information tools included with Windows 98.

Troubleshooting

When preparing for this objective domain, you will need a good understanding of the various diagnostic and troubleshooting utilities included with Windows 98. The potential errors encountered will dictate which set of tools you should use. For example, if there is a hardware conflict, you might start with the Device Manager and then move on to more advanced troubleshooting techniques, such as rebooting the system and manually loading device drivers. Tools such as PING and TRACERT can be used to help determine where network problems reside. You will also need to spend time understanding the process Windows 98 uses to install or upgrade the operating system. For example, if Setup crashes, you need to know that when you restart the system, the DETCRASH.LOG file is used so Setup knows to skip the hardware that caused the initial error. Using DETLOG.TXT, you can see the details of the success, or failure, of Setup after it finishes.

Tested Skills and Suggested Practices

The skills you need to successfully master the Troubleshooting Objective Domain on the exam include:

- **Using Windows 98 Setup.**

  - Practice 1: Install Windows 98 and review the resulting SETUPLOG.TXT located in the root C: drive.

  - Practice 2: Create and use an Emergency Startup Disk.

- **Using the System Configuration Utility.**

  - Practice 1: Start System Configuration Utility and practice backing up the system configuration files.

  - Practice 2: Using System Configuration Utility, limit the amount of memory used by Windows 98 to 4 MB.

- **Managing network resources.**

    - Practice 1: Install the Net Watcher utility.

    - Practice 2: Create a shared folder, connect to the folder from a remote computer, and use Net Watcher to verify the user name that has connected to this share.

- **Managing file systems.**

    - Practice 1: Start ScanDisk and check the status of the C: drive.

    - Practice 2: Using Disk Defragmenter, check the status of each fixed drive.

OBJECTIVE 6.1

Diagnose and resolve installation failures.

Windows 98 Setup includes a number of features to recover from installation failures. Depending on which phase causes Setup to fail, you can recover the installation process by turning the computer off and then back on. A common cause of Setup failing is a problem during the hardware detection phase. If a certain hardware device causes problems, Setup will skip that device when it restarts. You will then need to manually configure the device from the Device Manager.

In addition to detecting and resolving hardware configuration, Windows 98 includes a tool called the Version Conflict Manager (VCM). The VCM utility is used to correct potential shared-file problems. Windows 98 uses the same dynamic-link library (DLL) architecture as Windows 95. However, some DLLs have been upgraded with Windows 98. If a program that used to work under Windows 95 stops operating after installing Windows 98, the Version Conflict Manager should be run to resolve the problem.

To successfully answer the questions for this objective, you need a firm understanding of several key terms. For definitions of these terms, refer to the Glossary in this book.

Key Terms

- DETCRASH.LOG

- SETUPLOG.TXT

- Version Conflict Manager (VCM)

70-098.06.01.001

During a new installation of Windows 98, your computer locks up. You restart the computer by shutting it off, powering it back on, and continuing the Setup using Safe Recovery. The remainder of Setup continues without problems, but you notice that your network adapter is not functioning.

What is the most likely cause of this problem?

A. The network card should have been configured manually.

B. You should have restarted the computer using Ctrl+Alt+Del.

C. There was no cable connected to the network adapter during Setup.

D. Using the information in DETCRASH.LOG during Safe Recovery, Setup simply skipped loading any devices that failed to load the first time.

70-098.06.01.002

You just upgraded from Windows 95 to Windows 98. The upgrade completed without any problems. However, when you attempt to launch a Windows application that worked under Windows 95, the application no longer loads or functions.

How should you resolve this problem?

A. Rerun Windows 98 Setup and select Full Compatibility mode.

B. Upgrade the application to one that is compatible with Windows 98.

C. Reinstall the application to restore files overwritten by Windows 98.

D. Run Version Conflict Manager (VCM) to restore that application's files.

70-098.06.01.001

During a new installation of Windows 98, your computer locks up. You restart the computer by shutting it off, powering it back on, and continuing the Setup using Safe Recovery. The remainder of Setup continues without problems, but you notice that your network adapter is not functioning.

What is the most likely cause of this problem?

▶ **Correct Answer: D**

  A. **Incorrect.** Windows 98 will automatically detect network cards and install the appropriate driver. However, when you use Safe Recovery, Setup assumes that the autodetection completed successfully.

  B. **Incorrect.** If Setup crashes, you should turn the computer off and then on. Using Ctrl+Alt+Del will not reset the system for Setup to continue.

  C. **Incorrect.** A cable is not required for Windows 98 Setup to detect network cards.

  D. **Correct.** Safe Recovery uses DETCRASH.LOG to skip devices that may have caused Setup to fail. In this case, the network card was avoided when Setup resumed.

70-098.06.01.002

You just upgraded from Windows 95 to Windows 98. The upgrade completed without any problems. However, when you attempt to launch a Windows application that worked under Windows 95, the application no longer loads or functions.

How should you resolve this problem?

▶ **Correct Answer: D**

  A. **Incorrect.** You do not need to rerun Setup. Windows 98 includes the Version Conflict Manager to resolve problems like this.

  B. **Incorrect.** It is possible the application is compatible with Windows 98. Use the Version Conflict Manager to resolve the problem.

  C. **Incorrect.** You do not need to reinstall or restore any files because Windows 98 includes the Version Conflict Manager utility to correct problems that occur when upgrading from Windows 95.

  D. **Correct.** The Version Conflict Manager is provided to resolve file conflicts when upgrading from Windows 95 to Windows 98.

70-098.06.01.003

During the initial installation stage of Windows 98 Setup, your computer stops responding for a long period. What is the correct procedure for dealing with this?

A. Turn the computer off, then on, and rerun Setup.

B. Press Ctrl+Alt+Del to restart the computer and rerun Setup.

C. Press Ctrl+Alt+Del to restart the computer. Select Safe Recovery.

D. Turn the computer off, then on. When it restarts, Setup will resume automatically.

70-098.06.01.004

You have just completed Windows 98 Setup. During the installation, the system crashed twice. You examined your computer and noticed a number of files in the root of your C: drive that you have not seen before.

Which file records successfully completed detection steps so that Setup will not fail twice due to the same problem?

A. NETLOG.TXT

B. DETLOG.TXT

C. DETCRASH.LOG

D. SETUPLOG.TXT

70-098.06.01.003

During the initial installation stage of Windows 98 Setup, your computer stops responding for a long period. What is the correct procedure for dealing with this?

▶ **Correct Answer: A**

A. **Correct.** Only by turning the computer off and then back on can you be assured that all files associated with Setup are removed before running it again.

B. **Incorrect.** Only by turning the computer off and then back on can you be assured that all files associated with Setup have been removed.

C. **Incorrect.** The computer should be turned off and then on before resuming Setup.

D. **Incorrect.** Setup will not resume automatically. After turning the computer back on, you must restart Setup.

70-098.06.01.004

You have just completed Windows 98 Setup. During the installation, the system crashed twice. You examined your computer and noticed a number of files in the root of your C: drive that you have not seen before.

Which file records successfully completed detection steps so that Setup will not fail twice due to the same problem?

▶ **Correct Answer: C**

A. **Incorrect.** NETLOG.TXT is a text file that describes the detection results for network components during Windows 98 Setup. It is not used to aid Setup in avoiding a second possible failure.

B. **Incorrect.** DETLOG.TXT provides a log of the hardware that was detected by Setup. It does not prevent Setup from crashing in the same place.

C. **Correct.** Only DETCRASH.LOG will prevent the hardware detection feature of Setup from crashing on the same device a second time. If Setup must restart, Safe Recovery will use DETCRASH.LOG to skip whatever device failed the first time.

D. **Incorrect.** SETUPLOG.TXT is a log of information created by Setup during the installation process. It does not help Setup prevent crashing.

70-098.06.01.005

You are running Setup and it hangs during installation. You do not shut down and restart the computer; instead, you attempt to restart Setup. During this attempt, Setup fails and an error message appears.

What is the most likely cause of this error message?

A. Your system memory is corrupted.

B. SETUPX.DLL is still loaded in memory.

C. DETLOG.TXT cannot be found without rebooting the system.

D. DETCRASH.LOG cannot be found without rebooting the system.

70-098.06.01.005

You are running Setup and it hangs during installation. You do not shut down and restart the computer; instead, you attempt to restart Setup. During this attempt, Setup fails and an error message appears.

What is the most likely cause of this error message?

▶ **Correct Answer: B**

A. **Incorrect.** Memory is not corrupted. Instead, some files from Setup are still in memory, and only turning off the computer will remove them.

B. **Correct.** Only by turning off the computer and then turning it back on can you be assured that all files associated with Setup have been removed. Setup can then continue the installation process.

C. **Incorrect.** DETLOG.TXT is a log of hardware that was detected by Setup. It does not affect whether Setup fails.

D. **Incorrect.** DETCRASH.LOG is used by Safe Recovery and is created if and when Setup fails.

Further Reading

Microsoft Windows 98 Training Kit. Complete Lesson 5, "Troubleshooting Windows 98 Setup," of Chapter 2, "Installing Windows 98." In this lesson you will learn about the installation issues involved when setting up Windows 98.

Microsoft Windows 98 Resource Kit. Read pages 175–186 to learn more about the Windows 98 setup process.

Windows 98 Accelerated MCSE Study Guide. Read Chapter 4, "Installing Windows 98," to learn more about the Windows 98 installation process.

OBJECTIVE 6.2

Diagnose and resolve boot process failures.

Once Windows 98 has been installed and all hardware devices configured, a potential problem can be encountered when the user boots the system. When preparing for the exam, you should be aware of the steps that occur when booting Windows 98. If you understand this process, it will be easier to determine if a problem is hardware-related or software-related. Windows 98 includes various tools for determining the specific problem during startup. The Windows 98 boot process occurs in the following distinct stages:

- BIOS bootstrap

- Master Boot Record (MBR) and Boot Sector

- Real-mode boot

- Real-mode configuration

- Protected-mode load

You can control the boot process by editing the Options section of MSDOS.SYS in any text editor. Using the System Configuration Utility, you can back up and edit system files, and control and troubleshoot startup. In addition, the Windows 98 Startup menu provides a number of options to assist you in troubleshooting the boot process. For example, you can start your computer in safe mode, which loads only the mouse, keyboard, standard VGA, and other drivers that Device Manager needs to function. Another useful feature is Windows 98's ability to create a file called BOOTLOG.TXT, which records events that occur during the boot process. Use the BOOTLOG.TXT file to diagnose driver load failures and driver initialization failures.

If Windows 98 reports a corrupt registry, you can run the registry checker, called SCANREG, from a DOS prompt using the /FIX argument. Since you will not be able to load Windows 98, you will not be able to use the Windows version of the registry checker. You should also prepare an Emergency Startup Disk to help recover from serious problems, such as corrupted system files or system registry.

To successfully answer the questions for this objective, you need a firm understanding of several key terms. For definitions of these terms, refer to the Glossary in this book.

Key Terms

- Boot

- Emergency Startup Disk (ESD)

- Windows Registry Checker

70-098.06.02.001

After you start your Windows 98 computer, a warning dialog box displays on the screen indicating that the registry is corrupt. What should you do?

A. Continue to load Windows and run ScanDisk after booting up the computer.

B. Continue to load Windows and restore the system from tape.

C. Boot to a command prompt and run SCANREG. The Registry Checker will automatically repair the registry.

D. Boot to a command prompt and run SCANREG with the /RESTORE switch. You must then select a previously good registry to restore.

70-098.06.02.002

You are attempting a repair on a Windows 98 computer. After you boot the computer, Windows will not run. Windows 98 does not recognize the CD-ROM device installed on your computer, but you do have drivers for it.

The required result is to perform an emergency repair operation.

The first optional result is to avoid reinstalling Windows 98.

The second optional result is to be able to copy needed files from the Windows 98 CD.

You propose to copy the correct drivers for the CD-ROM device to the Emergency Startup Disk (ESD), edit the CONFIG.SYS file on the ESD so it will load the drivers, boot from the ESD, and re-store the files as needed from both the ESD and the Windows 98 CD-ROM.

What does the proposed solution provide?

A. The required result and all optional results.

B. The required result and one optional result.

C. The required result but none of the optional results.

D. The proposed solution does not provide the required result.

70-098.06.02.001

After you start your Windows 98 computer, a warning dialog box displays on the screen indicating that the registry is corrupt. What should you do?

▶ **Correct Answer: C**

   A. **Incorrect.** ScanDisk is used to repair file system errors on a hard drive. It will not repair or restore the system registry. Use the SCANREG utility instead.

   B. **Incorrect.** You do not need to restore the Windows 98 system from a backup. Instead use the SCANREG utility to fix the registry.

   C. **Correct.** SCANREG using the /FIX argument will repair the registry. However, this must be run from a command prompt.

   D. **Incorrect.** The proper argument for running SCANREG from a command prompt to repair a corrupt registry is /FIX.

70-098.06.02.002

You are attempting a repair on a Windows 98 computer. After you boot the computer, Windows will not run. Windows 98 does not recognize the CD-ROM device installed on your computer, but you do have drivers for it.

The required result is to perform an emergency repair operation.

The first optional result is to avoid reinstalling Windows 98.

The second optional result is to be able to copy needed files from the Windows 98 CD.

You propose to copy the correct drivers for the CD-ROM device to the Emergency Startup Disk (ESD), edit the CONFIG.SYS file on the ESD so it will load the drivers, boot from the ESD, and restore the files as needed from both the ESD and the Windows 98 CD-ROM.

What does the proposed solution provide?

▶ **Correct Answer: A**

   A. **Correct.** Using the ESD to install the CD-ROM drivers will allow you to install the necessary files from the Windows 98 CD and restore the system.

   B. **Incorrect.** Since the ESD is able to locate the Windows 98 CD-ROM, all results will be achieved.

   C. **Incorrect.** All results will be achieved since the ESD can now access the Windows 98 CD.

   D. **Incorrect.** All results will be achieved since the ESD can now access the Windows 98 CD.

70-098.06.02.003

Your computer runs an application that requires expanded memory but does not seem to be operating. What can be done to provide expanded memory support for this application?

A. Load the EMM386 device into the CONFIG.SYS file.

B. Configure EMS support in the MS-DOS configuration item in Control Panel.

C. Applications requiring expanded memory are not supported by Windows 98.

D. Create a Program Information File (PIF) and enable expanded memory support for that application.

70-098.06.02.004

Upon starting Windows 98, you receive the following message:

"Windows encountered an error accessing the system Registry. Windows will restart and repair the system for you now."

Which program is run when the system restarts?

A. SCANREG

B. DETECT.LOG

C. RegWizard

D. ScanRegW

E. DETECTLOG.TXT

70-098.06.02.003

Your computer runs an application that requires expanded memory but does not seem to be operating. What can be done to provide expanded memory support for this application?

▶ **Correct Answer: A**

A. **Correct.** By default, an expanded memory manager is not installed by Windows 98. However, you can manually add EMM386 to CONFIG.SYS.

B. **Incorrect.** You can add an expanded memory manager by editing the CONFIG.SYS file.

C. **Incorrect.** Windows 98 does not support applications that require an expanded memory manager unless a manager, such as EMM386, is first installed.

D. **Incorrect.** PIF files are not required by Windows 98. Instead, add the memory manager to the CONFIG.SYS file.

70-098.06.02.004

Upon starting Windows 98, you receive the following message:

"Windows encountered an error accessing the system Registry. Windows will restart and repair the system for you now."

Which program is run when the system restarts?

▶ **Correct Answer: A**

A. **Correct.** The SCANREG utility is used to fix problems encountered in the registry.

B. **Incorrect.** There is no file (or application) named DETECT.LOG in Windows 98. Instead, the Registry Checker, SCANREG, will be launched.

C. **Incorrect.** There is no application called RegWizard in Windows 98. SCANREG is used to repair problems with the registry.

D. **Incorrect.** ScanRegW is the Windows version of the Registry Checker. For repairing a corrupt registry, the DOS-based SCANREG utility will be run.

E. **Incorrect.** There is no file (or application) named DETECTLOG.TXT in Windows 98. Instead, the Registry Checker, SCANREG, will be launched.

Further Reading

Microsoft Windows 98 Training Kit. Complete Lesson 2, "Controlling and Trouble-shooting the Boot Process," of Chapter 10, "Troubleshooting Windows 98 in a Stand-alone Environment." In this lesson you will learn about the boot process and how to troubleshoot potential problems.

Microsoft Windows 98 Resource Kit. Read pages 175–186 to learn more about the Windows 98 boot process.

O B J E C T I V E   6 . 3

Diagnose and resolve connectivity problems in a Microsoft environment and a mixed Microsoft and NetWare environment.

The Windows 98 network troubleshooting tools that you will need to be familiar with include:

- Net Watcher

- PING

- TRACERT

- Winipcfg

When you're using TCP/IP, Winipcfg allows you to quickly determine the current protocol configuration. This includes both static IP information as well as settings provided by DHCP. You cannot change static TCP/IP settings with Winipcfg. However, in the event you are using DHCP, Winipcfg allows you to renew or release IP addresses that have been leased.

Like Winipcfg, Net Watcher is also a Windows-based utility. Net Watcher allows you to monitor access to shared resources. In addition, you can create, add, or delete shares on remote computers. Consider using Net Watcher when you need to determine which users are connected to specific shares.

PING and TRACERT are both DOS-based utilities that can help you verify network access when using TCP/IP. PING is used to verify that a path exists between your computer and a remote computer. The remote system can be on the local network or across the Internet. You can pass either a computer host name or IP address when you run PING. TRACERT will also verify a path exists between your computer and a remote computer. However, unlike PING, TRACERT will report information about the route used to get to the other system. In addition, TRACERT will report the time required to travel to the remote computer. Using TRACERT, you can determine network bottlenecks.

To successfully answer the questions for this objective, you need a firm understanding of several key terms. For definitions of these terms, refer to the Glossary in this book.

Key Terms

- PING

- TRACERT

- Winipcfg

70-098.06.03.001

A Windows 98 computer in your office is having trouble with its Internet connection. Your office is connected to the Internet through a proxy server. Which tool can you use to verify the connection to the proxy server by sending ICMP echo packets?

A. PING

B. TRACERT

C. Winipcfg

D. Ipconfig

E. Network Monitor

70-098.06.03.002

You are shutting down Windows 98 when the following message appears:

"There are 1 user(s) connected to your computer. Shutting down your computer will disconnect them. Do you want to continue?"

What is the best method to deal with this condition?

A. Right-click Network Neighborhood, select the resource in question, and choose Disconnect from the menu.

B. Open Net Watcher, and identify the user connected to the resource. Notify the user to close the file, and then shut down your computer.

C. Open System Monitor, and identify the resource in use. Select Disconnect User from the Administer menu. Windows 98 will automatically close the file properly.

D. Open Net Watcher, and identify the user connected to the resource. Select Disconnect User from the Administer menu. Windows 98 will automatically close the file properly.

70-098.06.03.001

A Windows 98 computer in your office is having trouble with its Internet connection. Your office is connected to the Internet through a proxy server. Which tool can you use to verify the connection to the proxy server by sending ICMP echo packets?

▶ **Correct Answer: A**

A. **Correct.** Using PING, you can send test packets to a remote IP address to verify a path exists between your computer and the remote computer. This can help diagnose potential problems with a proxy server.

B. **Incorrect.** TRACERT provides information about network paths but does not use ICMP echo packets to test the network.

C. **Incorrect.** Winipcfg will provide detailed information about the system's TCP/IP settings. This includes IP address and gateway information. However, use PING to verify the path from your computer to the proxy server.

D. **Incorrect.** Ipconfig, like Winipcfg, provides general information about the system's TCP/IP settings. However, use PING to get more information about the path used to access the Internet via a proxy server.

E. **Incorrect.** Network Monitor will not provide information about the system network configuration.

70-098.06.03.002

You are shutting down Windows 98 when the following message appears:

"There are 1 user(s) connected to your computer. Shutting down your computer will disconnect them. Do you want to continue?"

What is the best method to deal with this condition?

▶ **Correct Answer: B**

A. **Incorrect.** Since you do not know which user is currently connected, Network Neighborhood will not provide the information you need to warn the connected user.

B. **Correct.** Once you know which user is connected to your system, you can warn him to close any open files or save his work before restarting the system.

C. **Incorrect.** Only the user who has a file, or resource, in use can properly close the resource. Use Net Watcher to determine which user is accessing the system and warn him of the system status.

D. **Incorrect.** While Net Watcher will help you identify which user is accessing the system, you cannot properly close open files. The user will have to be notified of the system status and close any open files.

70-098.06.03.003

You attempt to connect to a server across your company's WAN and are unable to establish a session. You ping the name of the server, but receive the following response:

Pinging pharaoh.genesis.com [172.16.31.220] with 32 bytes of data:
Request timed out.
Request timed out.
Request timed out.
Request timed out.

Ping statistics for 172.16.31.220:
Packets: Sent = 4, Received = 0, Lost = 4 (100% loss),

Approximate round trip times in milli-seconds:
Minimum = 0ms, Maximum = 0ms, Average = 0ms

What is the next troubleshooting procedure?

A. Ping the local host.

B. Reboot your computer.

C. Ping the default gateway.

D. Release and renew your IP address.

70-098.06.03.004

What is an advantage of the TRACERT command over the PING command?

A. It is more secure than the PING utility.

B. It can be used through a proxy server when PING cannot.

C. It confirms the client's ability to establish a session with the host.

D. It returns the fully qualified domain name and IP address of each gateway along a route to a host.

70-098.06.03.003

You attempt to connect to a server across your company's WAN and are unable to establish a session. You ping the name of the server, but receive the following response:

Pinging pharaoh.genesis.com [172.16.31.220] with 32 bytes of data:
Request timed out.
Request timed out.
Request timed out.
Request timed out.

Ping statistics for 172.16.31.220:
Packets: Sent = 4, Received = 0, Lost = 4 (100% loss),

Approximate round trip times in milli-seconds:
Minimum = 0ms, Maximum = 0ms, Average = 0ms

What is the next troubleshooting procedure?

▶ **Correct Answer: C**

A. **Incorrect.** Testing whether you can ping your local host will not help you identify why you are unable to ping a remote system.

B. **Incorrect.** Since you are able to run PING, you will not be required to reboot your computer. Instead, verify that you can ping the gateway to the remote computer.

C. **Correct.** By testing your access to the gateway, you can verify that your system can send packets to remote networks. If this fails, you may need to check your local system or verify the gateway is active.

D. **Incorrect.** Obtaining a new IP address is not the next step. You should verify you can ping the gateway next.

70-098.06.03.004

What is an advantage of the TRACERT command over the PING command?

▶ **Correct Answer: D**

A. **Incorrect.** TRACERT is no more or less secure than PING. TRACERT does provide more information about the path your computer is using to access a remote computer. PING only reports if you can "see" the other system.

B. **Incorrect.** Neither TRACERT or PING can be used through a proxy.

C. **Incorrect.** TRACERT only provides a report on the path used to get to a remote system; it does not help you determine if you can access that system.

D. **Correct.** TRACERT provides details about the path used to "see" the other system. With this information, you can determine if the path is the most efficient.

70-098.06.03.005

You need to remotely view the registry of a Windows 98 computer on your network, but your attempts to view it have failed. Which components must be installed on both computers to allow this remote connection? (Choose two.)

A. TCP/IP

B. User-level access control

C. Microsoft Network Monitor Agent

D. Microsoft Remote Registry Service

E. File and Printer Sharing for Microsoft Networks

70-098.06.03.005

You need to remotely view the registry of a Windows 98 computer on your network, but your attempts to view it have failed. Which components must be installed on both computers to allow this remote connection? (Choose two.)

▶ **Correct Answers: B and D**

    A. **Incorrect.** TCP/IP is not required to access a remote computer's registry.

    B. **Correct.** Only with user-level security enabled can you allow remote users access to a local registry. The stability of the registry is critical for Windows 98 and should be controlled with the highest level of security.

    C. **Incorrect.** The Microsoft Network Monitor Agent does not allow remote users to access the registry. Instead, you must install Microsoft Remote Registry Service.

    D. **Correct.** In addition to user-level security, Microsoft Remote Registry Service is required on the host computer.

    E. **Incorrect.** While File and Printer Sharing for Microsoft Networks allows remote users access to local system resources, this does not include the registry.

Further Reading

Microsoft Windows 98 Training Kit. Complete Lesson 1, "Installing and Configuring Network Components," of Chapter 12, "Configuring Windows 98 for Use on a Network." In this lesson, network configuration options will be discussed.

Windows 98 Accelerated MCSE Study Guide. Read Chapter 8, "Network Configuration," to learn more about implementing network access from Windows 98.

OBJECTIVE 6.4

Diagnose and resolve printing problems in a Microsoft environment and a mixed Microsoft and NetWare environment.

Windows 98 can print to local printers or shared printers across a network. In addition, you can print from either Windows-based or DOS-based applications. To print from a DOS-based application, you must capture the port when configuring the printer driver. You need to do this whether the printer is local or remote.

During the process of printing to a remote printer on a Novell network, many of the printer's configuration items are stored in the server's bindery. When a Windows 98 client connects to a NetWare server, the drivers are retrieved. However, the Windows 98 computer must have Client for NetWare Networks installed to access one of these printers.

To successfully answer the questions for this objective, you need a firm understanding of several key terms. For definitions of these terms, refer to the Glossary in this book.

Key Terms

- Dial-Up Networking

- File and Printer Sharing for Microsoft Networks

- File and Printer Sharing for NetWare Networks

- Share-level security

- User-level security

70-098.06.04.001

When making a dial-up connection, you cannot access print queues on remote NetWare servers. Your computer is running File and Printer Sharing for NetWare. How can you resolve this problem?

A. Access control is set to share-level. Change the setting to user-level.

B. Set the IPX protocol to be the default protocol in the Network Control Panel.

C. Windows 98 does not support printing to NetWare printers over dial-up connections.

D. Disable File and Printer Sharing for NetWare Networks before you make the dial-up connection.

70-098.06.04.002

You are having problems printing to your local printer. When you print a large graphic image, only half of the page prints. What is causing the problem? (Choose two.)

A. Invalid font

B. Full printer spool

C. Incompatible printer

D. Insufficient printer memory

70-098.06.04.001

When making a dial-up connection, you cannot access print queues on remote NetWare servers. Your computer is running File and Printer Sharing for NetWare. How can you resolve this problem?

▶ **Correct Answer: D**

A. **Incorrect.** Because this is a NetWare network, the access control level is already set to user-level. However, this does not prevent you from accessing the print queues. You must first remove File and Printer Sharing for NetWare.

B. **Incorrect.** You do not have to set the IPX/SPX protocol to default in order to access remote shares or printer queues.

C. **Incorrect.** Windows 98 does support printing to remote NetWare printers when using Dial-Up Networking.

D. **Correct.** When using Dial-Up Networking, you need to first disable File and Printer Sharing for NetWare Networks if it is installed on the Windows 98 computer.

70-098.06.04.002

You are having problems printing to your local printer. When you print a large graphic image, only half of the page prints. What is causing the problem? (Choose two.)

▶ **Correct Answers: A and D**

A. **Correct.** If a page does not print properly, the fonts used could be part of the problem. Try printing the graphic from a different application, or change the fonts used.

B. **Incorrect.** The capacity of the printer spool will not affect whether the entire page prints.

C. **Incorrect.** An incompatible printer will not be able to print half the page.

D. **Correct.** If the printer does not have enough physical memory, it may not be able to completely print large graphics.

70-098.06.04.003

You are attempting to print from an MS-DOS-based program, but nothing prints on the network printer. You can print from Microsoft WordPad and other Windows-based programs. What is the most likely cause of the problem?

A. The printer is out of toner.

B. The printer is out of paper.

C. The printer port must be captured.

D. Windows 98 cannot print MS-DOS print jobs over the network.

70-098.06.04.004

You are trying to use Point and Print to install a printer. The printer is located on a NetWare 3.11 server using bindery emulation. How can you set up the server to enable Point and Print?

A. Point and Print cannot use bindery emulation. It can only use bindery.

B. The printer's name and configuration must be added to the server's bindery.

C. The name of the printer driver files must be configured in the server's bindery.

D. The location of the printer driver files must be configured in the server's bindery.

E. The Novell line of operating systems does not support Windows 98 Point and Print.

F. Point and Print can only use NDS with a NetWare 4.11 server for Point and Print capabilities.

70-098.06.04.003

You are attempting to print from an MS-DOS-based program, but nothing prints on the network printer. You can print from Microsoft WordPad and other Windows-based programs. What is the most likely cause of the problem?

▶ **Correct Answer: C**

A. **Incorrect.** A lack of toner will either print a page too lightly or not at all. You would not be able to print from any application if the printer were out of toner.

B. **Incorrect.** If the printer were out of paper, you would not be able to print from any application. Since you can print from some applications, there is another problem with the printer.

C. **Correct.** Windows 98 supports printing from Windows-based and DOS-based applications. However, the port must first be captured in order to print from DOS-based applications.

D. **Incorrect.** Windows 98 can print to local or network printers from DOS-based applications as long as the port has first been captured when configuring the printer driver.

70-098.06.04.004

You are trying to use Point and Print to install a printer. The printer is located on a NetWare 3.11 server using bindery emulation. How can you set up the server to enable Point and Print?

▶ **Correct Answers: B, C, and D**

A. **Incorrect.** Point and Print can use the NetWare server's bindery or bindery emulation.

B. **Correct.** Both the printer name and configuration must be saved in the NetWare server's bindery. However, the printer settings, such as paper size, will not be transferred to Windows 98.

C. **Correct.** In addition to the printer name and configuration, the driver name must also be stored in the bindery.

D. **Correct.** The printer's driver is retrieved by the Windows 98 client when connecting to the NetWare server. Therefore, the location of the files must also be saved in the bindery.

E. **Incorrect.** Novell networks do support Point and Print operations from a Windows 98 client.

F. **Incorrect.** Point and Print using NetWare Directory Services (NDS) can be used from NetWare 3.x servers as well as 4.11 servers.

70-098.06.04.005

You need to give a real-mode NetWare client access to a printer connected to a Windows 98 computer. File and Printer Sharing for NetWare Networks is installed on the computer and the printer is shared. The NetWare client cannot access the printer, but a NetWare 4.11 server can print to the printer.

How can you resolve this problem and allow the real-mode NetWare clients access to your printer?

A. Enable SAP advertising on File and Printer Sharing for NetWare Networks.

B. Enable domain advertising on File and Printer Sharing for NetWare Networks.

C. Enable broadcast advertising on File and Print Sharing for NetWare Networks.

D. Enable workgroup advertising on File and Printer Sharing for NetWare Networks.

70-098.06.04.005

You need to give a real-mode NetWare client access to a printer connected to a Windows 98 computer. File and Printer Sharing for NetWare Networks is installed on the computer and the printer is shared. The NetWare client cannot access the printer, but a NetWare 4.11 server can print to the printer.

How can you resolve this problem and allow the real-mode NetWare clients access to your printer?

▶ **Correct Answer: A**

A. **Correct.** The real-mode clients must be using NETX or VLM and therefore SAP must be enabled on File and Printer Sharing for NetWare Networks in order for NetWare clients to browse for the shared printer. Since the server can connect to the printer, it must be using a protected-mode client.

B. **Incorrect.** Only SAP and workgroup advertising is supported by File and Printer Sharing for NetWare Networks. Domain advertising is not supported.

C. **Incorrect.** Only SAP and workgroup advertising is supported by File and Printer Sharing for NetWare Networks. Broadcast advertising is not supported.

D. **Incorrect.** Workgroup advertising is only supported by Microsoft clients. Since the Novell clients are using real-mode clients, you need to enable SAP advertising.

Further Reading

Microsoft Windows 98 Training Kit. Complete Lesson 3, "Configuring and Managing a Local Printer," of Chapter 8, "Supporting Local Printers in Windows 98." In this lesson, setting up a local printer will be discussed.

Microsoft Windows 98 Training Kit. Complete Lesson 3, "Using Windows NT Network Resources," of Chapter 13, "Using Windows 98 on a Windows NT Network." In this lesson you will learn how Windows NT shares resources and various security implications.

Microsoft Windows 98 Resource Kit. Read pages 523–531 to learn more about troubleshooting printers and font problems.

Microsoft Windows 98 Resource Kit. Read pages 503–504 to learn more about configuring Point and Print capabilities using a Novell network.

Windows 98 Accelerated MCSE Study Guide. Read Chapter 11, "Printing," to learn more about configuring local and network printers.

O B J E C T I V E   6 . 5

Diagnose and resolve file system problems.

If you suspect file system problems, you can use the Windows-based or MS-DOS-based versions of ScanDisk. ScanDisk supports checking and repairing both FAT16 and FAT32 file systems. You can also use ScanDisk to check compressed drives. Remember, only FAT16 file systems can be compressed.

In addition to ScanDisk, Windows 98 also includes the Disk Defragmenter utility. This tool will defragment files on a hard drive. Over time, fragmented files can reduce the overall performance of the Windows 98 computer. Disk Defragmenter can also be used to optimize the startup time for applications.

To successfully answer the questions for this objective, you need a firm understanding of several key terms. For definitions of these terms, refer to the Glossary in this book.

Key Terms

- Disk Defragmenter

- FAT16

- FAT32

70-098.06.05.001

After upgrading Windows 95 to Windows 98, you decide to revert to Windows 95. During Windows 98 setup, you saved the current file system. Since installing Windows 98, you have converted your hard drive to FAT32. An attempt to revert to Windows 95 has already failed. What can you do to revert to Windows 95?

A. Run Disk Defragmenter and uninstall Windows 98.

B. Use the Windows 98 utility to convert back to FAT16. Uninstall Windows 98.

C. Compress the FAT32 volume, and move the free space to a FAT16 volume. Uninstall Windows 98.

D. You cannot revert to Windows 95. You must use Fdisk to format the partition, and install Windows 95 from scratch.

70-098.06.05.002

You have installed Windows 98 on a system with two partitions. During installation, only the D: drive was converted to FAT32. The FAT16 partition on the C: drive is running short of space, and you would like to compress the drive. How can you compress the C: drive?

A. Use DriveSpace3 to compress the C: drive.

B. Convert the D: drive back to FAT16. Then use DriveSpace3 to compress the C: drive.

C. It is not possible. Once a disk in the system is running FAT32, no other drives may use compression.

D. Convert the C: drive to FAT32. The optimization provided by the new file system will provide additional space comparable to compression.

70-098.06.05.001

After upgrading Windows 95 to Windows 98, you decide to revert to Windows 95. During Windows 98 setup, you saved the current file system. Since installing Windows 98, you have converted your hard drive to FAT32. An attempt to revert to Windows 95 has already failed. What can you do to revert to Windows 95?

▶ **Correct Answer: D**

    A. **Incorrect.** Once the file system has been converted to FAT32, you cannot revert to Windows 95. Disk Defragmenter and Uninstall cannot be used.

    B. **Incorrect.** There is no tool to convert the file system back to FAT16. You will need to use Fdisk and rebuild the file system.

    C. **Incorrect.** You cannot compress a FAT32 file system. In addition, you cannot revert to Windows 95 once a Windows 98 system has been converted to FAT32. You will need to use Fdisk and rebuild the file system.

    D. **Correct.** Once a system has been converted to FAT32, you will need to use Fdisk and rebuild the file system.

70-098.06.05.002

You have installed Windows 98 on a system with two partitions. During installation, only the D: drive was converted to FAT32. The FAT16 partition on the C: drive is running short of space, and you would like to compress the drive. How can you compress the C: drive?

▶ **Correct Answer: A**

    A. **Correct.** You can only compress FAT16 file systems. The FAT32 partition cannot be compressed.

    B. **Incorrect.** You cannot convert a FAT32 file system to FAT16. However, you can compress the C: drive since it is using FAT16.

    C. **Incorrect.** Drives that are using FAT16 can still be compressed. In this case, you can compress the C: drive to obtain additional drive space.

    D. **Incorrect.** Since you want to compress the drive, you should not convert it to FAT32. FAT32 file systems cannot be compressed.

70-098.06.05.003

You upgrade from Windows 95 OSR2 to Windows 98 and save system files during installation. After installing Windows 98, you converted the file system to FAT32. You want to restore Windows 95 OSR2. Which command will begin the restoration process?

A. Winundo.

B. Winrest.

C. Restore95.

D. Winundo98.

E. Windows 95 cannot be restored.

F. Uninstall Windows 98 from the Add/Remove programs utility.

70-098.06.05.003

You upgrade from Windows 95 OSR2 to Windows 98 and save system files during installation. After installing Windows 98, you converted the file system to FAT32. You want to restore Windows 95 OSR2. Which command will begin the restoration process?

▶ **Correct Answer: E**

A. **Incorrect.** Winundo is a data file used for restoring a previous version of Windows. It is not a command that can be run. In addition, since the Windows 98 file system was converted to FAT32, it cannot be restored to Windows 95.

B. **Incorrect.** Winrest is not a command supported by Windows 98. Since the file system was converted to FAT32, it cannot be restored to Windows 95.

C. **Incorrect.** Restore95 is not a command supported by Windows 98. Since the file system was converted to FAT32, it cannot be restored to Windows 95.

D. **Incorrect.** Winundo98 is not a command supported by Windows 98. Since the file system was converted to FAT32, it cannot be restored to Windows 95.

E. **Correct.** Since the file system was converted to FAT32 after Windows 98 was installed, Windows 95 cannot be restored. Only if the file system was originally FAT32 could you return to the previous version of Windows.

F. **Incorrect.** Since the file system was converted to FAT32 after installing Windows 98, you cannot uninstall Windows.

70-098.06.05.004

You are at a command prompt and need to access a file named MANAGEMENT_14.WPD. This is the fourteenth sequential file created on this partition. How will the long filename be truncated when it is the fourteenth sequential file?

A. MANA_14.WPG

B. MANA~14.WPD

C. MANAG~14.WPD

D. MANAG_14.WPD

E. MANA~_14.WPD

70-098.06.05.005

A user has a 2-GB FAT16 partition with 1 GB of free space. An attempt to save a document to the root directory failed. What likely caused the attempt to fail?

A. The user does not have access rights to the hard drive.

B. A user profile prevents the user from saving information to the hard disk.

C. Long filenames have taken up multiple directory entries, and the root directory is at its 512 maximum entries.

D. Long filenames have taken up multiple directory entries, and the root directory is at its 65,535 maximum entries.

70-098.06.05.004

You are at a command prompt and need to access a file named MANAGEMENT_14.WPD. This is the fourteenth sequential file created on this partition. How will the long filename be truncated when it is the fourteenth sequential file?

▶ **Correct Answer: C**

A. **Incorrect.** A tilde is used when long filenames are truncated, not an underscore. In addition, the first five characters are used from the filename, not the first four.

B. **Incorrect.** The first five characters are used when long filenames are truncated, not the first four.

C. **Correct.** The first five characters are used when truncating a long filename, and then a tilde is added before a sequential number is used.

D. **Incorrect.** A tilde, not an underscore, is used when truncating a long filename.

E. **Incorrect.** The first five characters are used when long filenames are truncated, and only the tilde is added, not an underscore.

70-098.06.05.005

A user has a 2-GB FAT16 partition with 1 GB of free space. An attempt to save a document to the root directory failed. What likely caused the attempt to fail?

▶ **Correct Answer: C**

A. **Incorrect.** When using Windows 98, all users will have access to the hard drive. For increased control over access, consider using Windows NT with an NTFS file system.

B. **Incorrect.** User profiles cannot prohibit a user from accessing the hard drive.

C. **Correct.** Root directories have a limit of 512 entries. Also, remember that long filenames require more than one entry in the directory. You will need to reorganize the folders currently existing in the root directory.

D. **Incorrect.** With FAT16, the directory limit is 512 entries, not 65,535 as with FAT32. You will need to reorganize the folders currently existing in the root directory.

Further Reading

Microsoft Windows 98 Training Kit. Complete Lesson 2, "Performing Maintenance Tasks," of Chapter 9, "Maintaining Windows 98 in a Stand-alone Environment." In this lesson, various maintenance tools, such as Disk Cleanup, will be discussed.

Windows 98 Accelerated MCSE Study Guide. Read Chapter 5, "Disk Management," to learn more about managing hard drives and file systems.

Diagnose and resolve resource access problems in a Microsoft environment and a mixed Microsoft and NetWare environment.

When attempting to access NetWare resources, Windows 98 must have the Client for NetWare Networks component installed. When you install this component, the required Novell IPX/SPX protocol will be installed as well. To access a Microsoft network, you will need to install the Client for Microsoft Networks components. Windows 98 supports running both of these components at the same time.

To share local resources with a NetWare client, you must install and configure File and Printer Sharing for NetWare Networks. NetWare uses user-level access, so a security provider must exist before Windows 98 will allow access to its resources. In addition, you cannot run both the Microsoft and NetWare file and print sharing components at the same time.

To successfully answer the questions for this objective, you need a firm understanding of several key terms. For definitions of these terms, refer to the Glossary in this book.

Key Terms

- Client for NetWare Networks

- File and Printer Sharing for NetWare Networks

- IPX/SPX protocol

- Primary Domain Controller (PDC)

70-098.06.06.001

Five new Windows 98 computers are added to your department. The primary users of these computers need to store files on a NetWare server. However, they cannot see resources on the NetWare server. They can print to a shared printer on a Windows NT Workstation 4.0 computer in their group.

Which single step will solve this problem?

A. Install the IPX/SPX protocol on the new computers.

B. Install Client for NetWare Networks on the new computers.

C. Install Gateway Services for NetWare on a Windows NT server.

D. Install File and Printer Sharing for NetWare on a Windows NT server.

70-098.06.06.002

A company's network has 2 NetWare 3.12 servers, 3 Windows NT 4.0 servers, and 80 Windows 98 computers. Numerous Windows 98 network computers cannot run NetBIOS-based applications, but file transfers are functioning normally. The only network protocol on any computer is either IPX/SPX or the Microsoft equivalent.

What can cause the Windows 98 computers not to be able to run NetBIOS-based applications?

A. The IPX/SPX frame type does not match on the computers.

B. The routers are not configured to pass Type 20 NetBIOS IPX packets.

C. The IPX/SPX-compatible protocol does not support NetBIOS applications.

D. The IPX/SPX protocol cannot be used on a Windows NT Server 4.0 domain.

70-098.06.06.001

Five new Windows 98 computers are added to your department. The primary users of these computers need to store files on a NetWare server. However, they cannot see resources on the NetWare server. They can print to a shared printer on a Windows NT Workstation 4.0 computer in their group.

Which single step will solve this problem?

▶ **Correct Answer: B**

   A. **Incorrect.** Client for NetWare Networks must be installed before Windows 98 can access NetWare network resources. IPX/SPX will be installed automatically if it is not currently installed.

   B. **Correct.** Client for NetWare Networks will allow Windows 98 clients the ability to access Novell resources.

   C. **Incorrect.** Windows 98 provides the Client for NetWare Networks component to access Novell resources. A Windows NT server is not required.

   D. **Incorrect.** File and Printer Sharing for NetWare is configured on a Windows 98 computer but is not required to access remote Novell resources.

70-098.06.06.002

A company's network has 2 NetWare 3.12 servers, 3 Windows NT 4.0 servers, and 80 Windows 98 computers. Numerous Windows 98 network computers cannot run NetBIOS-based applications, but file transfers are functioning normally. The only network protocol on any computer is either IPX/SPX or the Microsoft equivalent.

What can cause the Windows 98 computers not to be able to run NetBIOS-based applications?

▶ **Correct Answer: B**

   A. **Incorrect.** The frame type does not have to be configured manually when using IPX/SPX.

   B. **Correct.** Any routers on the network must be allowed to pass NetBIOS packets.

   C. **Incorrect.** IPX/SPX does support NetBIOS applications. The problem resides in how the routers are configured.

   D. **Incorrect.** IPX/SPX can be used with Windows NT Server and on a Microsoft network.

70-098.06.06.003

Several Windows 98 computers on your network are properly validated during logon, but fail to execute the Windows NT logon script. What is the most likely cause of this problem?

A. The logon script is not in the NETLOGON share of the Windows NT server.

B. The Windows 98 computer is not connected to the Primary Domain Controller.

C. The network logon scripts in a DOS window are not supported in Windows 98.

D. The local cached password on the Windows 98 computer does not match the network logon.

70-098.06.06.004

A NetWare 3.11 server cannot access a Windows 98 computer. The Windows 98 computer is running File and Printer Sharing for NetWare Networks. What is likely preventing the NetWare server from accessing the Windows 98 computer?

A. The security provider is not available.

B. The IPX/SPX-compatible protocol is not on the Windows 98 computer.

C. The Microsoft Client for NetWare Networks is not installed on the computer.

D. The Service for NetWare Directory Services must be installed on the Windows 98 computer.

70-098.06.06.003

Several Windows 98 computers on your network are properly validated during logon, but fail to execute the Windows NT logon script. What is the most likely cause of this problem?

▶ **Correct Answer: A**

A. **Correct.** Since users are being validated, the Windows 98 clients have access to the PDC. However, check if the logon script resides in the NETLOGON share on the Windows NT server.

B. **Incorrect.** Since the users are validated, they are able to access a Primary Domain Controller (PDC). The problem is where the logon script resides on the server.

C. **Incorrect.** Windows 98 supports network logon scripts.

D. **Incorrect.** If there were a password problem, the user would not be validated. Since users are being validated, the problem resides with the location of the logon script.

70-098.06.06.004

A NetWare 3.11 server cannot access a Windows 98 computer. The Windows 98 computer is running File and Printer Sharing for NetWare Networks. What is likely preventing the NetWare server from accessing the Windows 98 computer?

▶ **Correct Answer: A**

A. **Correct.** Novell resources are managed by user-level access. If a security provider is not available, Windows 98 cannot allow access to its shared resources.

B. **Incorrect.** Since File and Printer Sharing for NetWare Networks is installed, the IPX/SPX protocol is installed automatically.

C. **Incorrect.** Since File and Printer Sharing for NetWare Networks is installed, the Client for NetWare Networks component is installed.

D. **Incorrect.** You do not need NDS installed in order to allow NetWare servers access to shared resources.

Further Reading

Microsoft Windows 98 Training Kit. Complete Lesson 3, "Using Windows NT Network Resources," of Chapter 13, "Using Windows 98 on a Windows NT Network." In this lesson you will learn how Windows NT shares resources and various security implications.

Microsoft Windows 98 Training Kit. Complete Lesson 4, "Sharing Resources with NetWare Users," of Chapter 14, "Using Windows 98 on a Novell Network." In this lesson, using File and Printer Sharing for NetWare Networks will be discussed.

Windows 98 Accelerated MCSE Study Guide. Read Chapter 9, "Network Security," to learn more about implementing network access.

OBJECTIVE 6.7

Diagnose and resolve hardware device and device driver problems.

Windows 98 includes a number of tools for diagnosing hardware device problems. Use the Device Manager or the System Information Utility to begin troubleshooting problems with new devices, such as conflicts caused when a new device is added to the system. You can also use the Automatic Skip Driver Agent to narrow the field of device drivers that are possibly causing conflicts.

Each time Windows 98 boots, a backup of the registry is made automatically. If you suspect a problem with the registry, you can run the Windows Registry Checker, ScanRegW. The Registry Checker will also allow you to manually create a backup of the registry. In the event Windows 98 will not boot due to a corrupt registry, you can run the DOS-based registry checker called SCANREG. Use the /FIX argument to repair a corrupt registry from a DOS prompt.

When preparing for the exam, you should also have a good understanding of the processes Windows 98 uses when booting. For example, you should be familiar with boot files such as IO.SYS and WIN.COM.

To successfully answer the questions for this objective, you need a firm understanding of several key terms. For definitions of these terms, refer to the Glossary in this book.

Key Terms

- Device Manager

- IO.SYS

- System Information Utility

- Windows Registry Checker

70-098.06.07.001

During a check of your system, you run the MEM command from the command prompt and notice that both HIMEM.SYS and IFSHLP.SYS are loaded. You do not find a CONFIG.SYS file in the system anywhere. Why are these modules in memory? (Choose two.)

A. The files are automatically loaded by IO.SYS.

B. CONFIG.SYS is a hidden file and cannot be viewed from Explorer.

C. The files are loaded automatically by Windows 98 during real-mode boot.

D. The files are loaded automatically by Windows 98 during protected-mode boot.

70-098.06.07.002

What is loaded by WIN.COM?

A. Additional files as specified in CONFIG.SYS.

B. Kernel, GDI, and User libraries along with the Explorer shell.

C. WIN32.EXE and other virtual device drivers specified by the registry.

D. VMM32.VXD and other virtual device drivers specified by the registry.

70-098.06.07.001

During a check of your system, you run the MEM command from the command prompt and notice that both HIMEM.SYS and IFSHLP.SYS are loaded. You do not find a CONFIG.SYS file in the system anywhere. Why are these modules in memory? (Choose two.)

▶ **Correct Answers: A and C**

A. **Correct.** IO.SYS controls what drivers are loaded. This file replaces the MS-DOS IO.SYS and MSDOS.SYS files. You can, however, continue to use CONFIG.SYS for backward compatibility.

B. **Incorrect.** CONFIG.SYS is not hidden and can still be used. However, IO.SYS now provides this functionality.

C. **Correct.** When Windows 98 is booted in real mode, these files are automatically loaded into memory.

D. **Incorrect.** These files are only loaded automatically during a real-mode boot, not a protected-mode boot.

70-098.06.07.002

What is loaded by WIN.COM?

▶ **Correct Answer: D**

A. **Incorrect.** WIN.COM is used to load virtual device drivers required by the registry.

B. **Incorrect.** WIN.COM loads VMM32.VXD and various device drivers, not libraries or the Explorer shell.

C. **Incorrect.** While WIN.COM does load virtual device drivers, it does not load WIN32.EXE. Instead, WIN.COM loads VMM32.VXD.

D. **Correct.** WIN.COM loads VMM32.VXD and virtual device drivers as required by the registry.

70-098.06.07.003

You suspect a device driver is creating an initialization problem with your computer, and you need to find out which one. You decide to reboot the computer and selectively load and confirm the files to process. What is the preferred method to selectively load and confirm which files are processed?

A. Edit MSDOS.SYS.

B. Press F5 upon startup and choose Confirm Driver Load.

C. Run the System Configuration Utility and choose Selective Startup.

D. Run the System Configuration Utility and choose Diagnostic Startup.

70-098.06.07.004

A new sound card fails to function after you install it in your computer. You suspect a device conflict. Which tools should be used to identify and modify the conflict? (Choose two.)

A. System Monitor

B. Device Manager

C. System Information Utility

D. Control Panel/Multimedia configuration utility

70-098.06.07.003

You suspect a device driver is creating an initialization problem with your computer, and you need to find out which one. You decide to reboot the computer and selectively load and confirm the files to process. What is the preferred method to selectively load and confirm which files are processed?

▶ **Correct Answer: D**

    A. **Incorrect.** MSDOS.SYS has been replaced by IO.SYS. You should not edit IO.SYS to control what drivers are loaded.

    B. **Incorrect.** You should restart the system using Diagnostic Startup to selectively load and confirm files.

    C. **Incorrect.** Selective Startup only allows you to select basic files when starting Windows 98. Diagnostic Startup allows you to confirm each individual file, including device drivers, as it loads. Therefore, Selective Startup is not the correct choice.

    D. **Correct.** Diagnostic Startup will allow you to selectively choose which files, including device drivers, should be loaded as Windows 98 boots.

70-098.06.07.004

A new sound card fails to function after you install it in your computer. You suspect a device conflict. Which tools should be used to identify and modify the conflict? (Choose two.)

▶ **Correct Answers: B and C**

    A. **Incorrect.** The System Monitor will provide real-time feedback on the performance of Windows 98. To check on device conflicts, use the Device Manager or the System Information Utility.

    B. **Correct.** Using the Device Manager, you can check which hardware devices are in conflict, remove a device, or reinstall drivers for a particular hardware device.

    C. **Correct.** The Windows 98 System Information Utility can be used to diagnose hardware conflicts.

    D. **Incorrect.** The Multimedia tool in Control Panel can be used to configure multimedia devices, but it is not used to troubleshoot or resolve conflicts with other devices in the system. Use the Device Manager or the System Information Utility to reconfigure conflicting devices.

70-098.06.07.005

A Windows 98 computer, configured for multiple display, has three video cards and monitors connected to it. The three displays work well with Microsoft Excel and Access, but only the primary display works on a certain full-screen MS-DOS application. What can the user do to resolve this problem?

A. Switch the order of the PCI adapters on the motherboard.

B. Configure the MS-DOS settings to support multiple displays.

C. Confirm the device has been activated through the Display Properties.

D. A single screen is the only way a full-screen MS-DOS application will run.

70-098.06.07.005

A Windows 98 computer, configured for multiple display, has three video cards and monitors connected to it. The three displays work well with Microsoft Excel and Access, but only the primary
display works on a certain full-screen MS-DOS application. What can the user do to resolve this
problem?

▶ **Correct Answer: D**

    A. **Incorrect.** Since Windows 98 only supports full-screen DOS applications on the primary display,
the order of the PCI adapters is not relevant.

    B. **Incorrect.** Full-screen DOS applications cannot run on multiple displays. They can only appear on
a single monitor.

    C. **Incorrect.** Since full-screen DOS applications will only run on a single monitor, there are no set-
tings available to change this.

    D. **Correct.** Windows 98 will only present full-screen DOS applications on a single monitor.

Further Reading

Microsoft Windows 98 Training Kit. Complete Lesson 1, "Viewing System Information," of Chapter 9, "Maintaining Windows 98 in a Stand-alone Environment." In this lesson, the System Information Utility will be discussed.

Microsoft Windows 98 Training Kit. Complete Lesson 3, "Resolving Hardware Conflicts," of Chapter 10, "Troubleshooting Windows 98 in a Stand-alone Environment." In this lesson you will learn how to troubleshoot hardware conflicts using the Device Manager and the Automatic Skip Driver Agent.

Microsoft Windows 98 Training Kit. Complete Lesson 1, "Installing and Configuring Network Components," of Chapter 12, "Configuring Windows 98 for Use on a Network." In this lesson, setting up support for a TCP/IP network will be discussed.

Windows 98 Accelerated MCSE Study Guide. Read Chapter 6, "Hardware Configuration," to learn more about setting up hardware devices with Windows 98.

The Microsoft Certified Professional Program

The Microsoft Certified Professional (MCP) program is designed to comprehensively assess and maintain software-related skills. Microsoft has developed several certifications to provide industry recognition of a candidate's knowledge and proficiency with Microsoft products and technologies. This appendix provides suggestions to help you prepare for an MCP exam and describes the process for taking the exam. The appendix also contains an overview of the benefits associated with certification and gives you an example of the exam track you might take for MCSE certification.

Preparing for an MCP Exam

This section contains tips and information to help you prepare for an MCP certification exam. Besides study and test-taking tips, this section provides information on how and where to register, test fees, and what to expect upon arrival at the testing center.

Studying for an Exam

The best way to prepare for an MCP exam is to study, learn, and master the technology or operating system on which you will be tested. The Readiness Review can help complete your understanding of the software or technology by assessing your practical knowledge and helping you focus on additional areas of study. For example, if you are pursuing the Microsoft Certified Systems Engineer (MCSE) certification, you must learn and use the tested Microsoft operating system. You can then use the Readiness Review to understand the skills that test your knowledge of the operating system, perform suggested practices with the operating system, and ascertain additional areas where you should focus your study by using the electronic assessment.

▶ **To prepare for any certification exam**

1. Identify the objectives for the exam.

   The Readiness Review lists and describes the objectives you will be tested on during the exam.

2. Assess your current mastery of those objectives.

   The Readiness Review electronic assessment tool is a great way to test your grasp of the objectives.

3. Practice the job skills for the objectives you have not mastered, and read more information about the subjects tested in each of these objectives.

   You can take the electronic assessment multiple times until you feel comfortable with the subject material.

Your Practical Experience

MCP exams test the specific skills needed on the job. Since in the real world you are rarely called upon to recite a list of facts, the exams go beyond testing your knowledge of a product or terminology. Instead, you are asked to *apply* your knowledge to a situation, analyze a technical problem, and decide on the best solution. Your hands-on experience with the software and technology will greatly enhance your performance on the exam.

Test Registration and Fees

You can schedule your exam up to six weeks in advance, or as late as one working day before the exam date. Sylvan Prometric and Virtual University Enterprises (VUE) administer all the Microsoft Certified Professional exams. To take an exam at an authorized Prometric Testing Center, in the United States call Sylvan at 800-755-EXAM (3926). To register online, or for more registration information, visit Sylvan's Web site at http://www.slspro.com. For information about taking exams at a VUE testing center, visit the VUE information page at http://www.vue.com, or call 888-837-8616 in the United States. When you register, you will need the following information:

- Unique identification number (This is usually your Social Security or Social Insurance number. The testing center also assigns an identification number, which provides another way to distinguish your identity and test records.)

- Mailing address and phone number

- E-mail address

- Organization or company name

- Method of payment (Payment must be made in advance, usually with a credit card or check.)

Testing fees vary from country to country, but in the United States and many other countries the exams cost approximately $100 (U.S.). Contact the testing vendor for exact pricing. Prices are subject to change, and in some countries, additional taxes may be applied.

When you schedule the exam, you will be provided with instructions regarding the appointment, cancellation procedures, identification requirements, and information about the testing center location.

Taking an Exam

If this is your first Microsoft certification exam, you may find the following information helpful upon arrival at the testing center.

Arriving at Testing Center

When you arrive at the testing center, you will be asked to sign a log book and show two forms of identification, including one photo identification (such as a driver's license or company security identification). Before you may take the exam, you will be asked to sign a Non-Disclosure Agreement and a Testing Center Regulations form, which explains the rules you will be expected to comply with during the test. Upon leaving the exam room at the end of the test, you will again sign the log book.

Exam Details

Before you begin the exam, the test administrator will provide detailed instructions about how to complete the exam and how to use the testing computer or software. Because the exams are timed, if you have any questions, ask the exam administrator before the exam begins. Consider arriving 10 to 15 minutes early so you will have time to relax and ask questions before the exam begins. Some exams may include additional materials or exhibits (such as diagrams). If any exhibits are required for your exam, the test administrator will provide you with them before you begin the exam and collect them from you at the end of the exam.

The exams are all closed book. You may not use a laptop computer or have any notes or printed material with you during the exam session. You will be provided with a set amount of blank paper for use during the exam. All paper will be collected from you at the end of the exam.

The Exam Tutorial

The test administrator will show you to your test computer and will handle any preparations necessary to start the testing tool and display the exam on the computer. Before you begin your exam, you can take the exam tutorial which is designed to familiarize you with computer-administered tests by offering questions similar to those on the exam. Taking the tutorial does not affect your allotted time for the exam.

Exam Length and Available Time

The number of questions on each exam varies, as does the amount of time allotted for each exam. Generally, certification exams consist of 50 to 70 questions and take approximately 90 minutes to complete. Specific information about the number of exam questions and available time will be provided to you when you register.

Tips for Taking the Exam

Since the testing software lets you move forward and backward through the exam, answer the easy questions first. Then go back and spend the remaining time on the harder questions.

When answering the multiple-choice questions, eliminate the obviously incorrect answers first. There are no trick questions on the test, so the correct answer will always be among the list of possible answers.

Answer all the questions before you quit the exam. An unanswered question is scored as an incorrect answer. If you are unsure of the answer, make an educated guess.

Your Rights as a Test Taker

As an exam candidate, you are entitled to the best support and environment possible for your exam. In particular, you are entitled to a quiet, uncluttered test environment and knowledgeable and professional test administrators. You should not hesitate to ask the administrator any questions before the exam begins, and you should also be given time to take the online testing tutorial. Before leaving, you should be given the opportunity to submit comments about the testing center, staff, or about the test itself.

Getting Your Exam Results

After you have completed an exam, you will immediately receive your score online and be given a printed Examination Score Report, which also breaks down the results by section. Passing scores on the different certification exams vary. You do not need to send these scores to Microsoft. The test center automatically forwards them to Microsoft within five working days, and if you pass the exam, Microsoft sends a confirmation to you within two to four weeks.

If you do not pass a certification exam, you may call the testing vendor to schedule a time to retake the exam. Before reexamination, you should review the appropriate sections of the Readiness Review and focus additional study on the topic areas where your exam results could be improved. Please note that you must pay the full registration fee again each time you retake an exam.

About the Exams

Microsoft Certified Professional exams follow recognized standards for validity and reliability. They are developed by technical experts who receive input from job-function and technology experts.

How MCP Exams Are Developed

To ensure the validity and reliability of the certification exams, Microsoft adheres to a rigorous exam-development process that includes an analysis of the tasks performed in specific job functions. Microsoft then translates the job tasks into a comprehensive set of objectives which measure knowledge, problem-solving abilities, and skill level. The objectives are prioritized and then reviewed by technical experts to create the certification exam questions. (These objectives are also the basis for developing the Readiness Review series.) Technical and job-function experts review the exam objectives and questions several times before releasing the final exam.

Computer Adaptive Testing

Microsoft is developing more effective ways to determine who meets the criteria for certification by introducing innovative testing technologies. One of these testing technologies is computer adaptive testing (CAT). This testing method is currently available on a few certification exams and may not be available for the exam for which you are currently studying. When taking this exam, test takers start with an easy-to-moderate question. Those who answer the question correctly get a more difficult follow-up question. If that question is answered correctly, the difficulty of the subsequent question also increases. Conversely, if the first question is answered incorrectly, the following question will be easier. This process continues until the testing system determines the test taker's ability.

With this system, everyone may answer the same percentage of questions correctly, but because people with a higher ability can answer more difficult questions correctly, they will receive a higher score. To learn more about computer adaptive testing and other testing innovations, visit http://www.microsoft.com/mcp.

If You Have a Concern About the Exam Content

Microsoft Certified Professional exams are developed by technical and testing experts, with input and participation from job-function and technology experts.

Microsoft ensures that the exams adhere to recognized standards for validity and reliability. Candidates generally consider them to be relevant and fair. If you feel that an exam question is inappropriate or if you believe the correct answer shown to be incorrect, write or call Microsoft at the e-mail address or phone number listed for the Microsoft Certified Professional Program in the "References" section of this appendix.

Although Microsoft and the exam administrators are unable to respond to individual questions and issues raised by candidates, all input from candidates is thoroughly researched and taken into consideration during development of subsequent versions of the exams. Microsoft is committed to ensuring the quality of these exams, and your input is a valuable resource.

Overview of the MCP Program

Becoming a Microsoft Certified Professional is the best way to show employers, clients, and colleagues that you have the knowledge and skills required by the industry. Microsoft's certification program is one of the industry's most comprehensive programs for assessing and maintaining software-related skills, and the MCP designation is recognized by technical managers worldwide as a mark of competence.

Certification Programs

Microsoft offers a variety of certifications so you can choose the one that meets your job needs and career goals. The MCP program focuses on measuring a candidate's ability to perform a specific job function, such as one performed by a systems engineer or a solution developer. Successful completion of the certification requirements indicates your expertise in the field. Microsoft certifications include:

- Microsoft Certified Systems Engineer (MCSE)

- Microsoft Certified Systems Engineer + Internet (MCSE + I)

- Microsoft Certified Professional (MCP)

- Microsoft Certified Professional + Internet (MCP + I)

- Microsoft Certified Professional + Site Building

- Microsoft Certified Database Administrator (MCDBA)

- Microsoft Certified Solution Developer (MCSD)

Microsoft Certified Systems Engineer (MCSE)

Microsoft Certified Systems Engineers have a high level of expertise with Microsoft Windows NT and the Microsoft BackOffice integrated family of server software and can plan, implement, maintain, and support information systems with these products. MCSEs are required to pass four operating system exams and two elective exams. The Windows 98 (70-098) exam earns core credit toward this certification.

MCSE Exam Requirements

You can select a Microsoft Windows NT 3.51 or Microsoft Windows NT 4.0 track for the MCSE certification. From within the track you have selected, you must pass four core operating system exams and then pass two elective exams. Visit the Microsoft Certified Professional Web site for details about current exam requirements, exam alternatives, and retired exams. This roadmap outlines the path an MCSE candidate would pursue for Windows NT 4.0.

Microsoft Windows NT 4.0 Core Exams

You must pass four core exams and two elective exams. You may choose between Windows 95, Windows NT Workstation 4.0, or Windows 98 for one of the core exams. The core exams are as follows:

- Exam 70-067: Implementing and Supporting Microsoft Windows NT Server 4.0

- Exam 70-068: Implementing and Supporting Microsoft Windows NT Server 4.0 in the Enterprise

- Exam 70-064: Implementing and Supporting Microsoft Windows 95, or exam 70-073: Microsoft Windows NT Workstation 4.0, or exam 70-098: Implementing and Supporting Microsoft Windows 98

- Exam 70-058: Networking Essentials

MCSE Electives

The elective exams you choose are the same for all Windows NT tracks. You must choose two exams from the following list.

- Exam 70-013: Implementing and Supporting Microsoft SNA Server 3.0, or exam 70-085: Implementing and Supporting Microsoft SNA Server 4.0 (If both SNA Server exams are passed, only one qualifies as an MCSE elective.)

- Exam 70-018: Implementing and Supporting Microsoft Systems Management Server 1.2, or exam 70-019: Designing and Implementing Data Warehouses with Microsoft SQL Server 7.0, or exam 70-086: Implementing and Supporting Microsoft Systems Management Server 2.0 (If both SMS exams are passed, only one qualifies as an MCSE elective.)

- Exam 70-021: Microsoft SQL Server 4.2 Database Implementation, or exam 70-027: Implementing a Database Design on Microsoft SQL Server 6.5, or exam 70-029: Implementing a Database Design on Microsoft SQL Server 7.0 (If more than one SQL Server exam is passed, only one qualifies as an MCSE elective. Also note that exam 70-021 is scheduled to be retired in 1999.)

- Exam 70-022: Microsoft SQL Server 4.2 Database Administration for Microsoft Windows NT, exam 70-026: System Administration for Microsoft SQL Server 6.5, or exam 70-028: System Administration for Microsoft SQL Server 7.0 (If more than one exam is passed from this group, only one would qualify as an MCSE elective. Also note that exam 70-022 is scheduled to be retired in 1999.)

- Exam 70-053: Internetworking Microsoft TCP/IP on Microsoft Windows NT (3.5–3.51), or exam 70-059: Internetworking with Microsoft TCP/IP on Microsoft Windows NT 4.0 (If both exams are passed, only one would qualify as an MCSE elective.)

- Exam 70-056: Implementing and Supporting Web Sites Using Microsoft Site Server 3.0

- Exam 70-076: Implementing and Supporting Microsoft Exchange Server 5, or exam 70-081: Implementing and Supporting Microsoft Exchange Server 5.5 (If more than one of these exams is passed, only one would qualify as an MCSE elective.)

- Exam 70-077: Implementing and Supporting Microsoft Internet Information Server 3.0 and Microsoft Index Server 1.1, or exam 70-087: Implementing and Supporting Microsoft Internet Information Server 4.0 (If both exams are passed, only one would qualify as an MCSE elective.)

- Exam 70-078: Implementing and Supporting Microsoft Proxy Server 1.0, or exam 70-088: Implementing and Supporting Microsoft Proxy Server 2.0 (If both exams are passed, only one would qualify as an MCSE elective.)

- Exam 70-079: Implementing and Supporting Microsoft Internet Explorer 4.0 by Using the Internet Explorer Administration Kit

Note that certification requirements may change. In addition, some retired certification exams may qualify for credit towards current certification programs. For the latest details on core and elective exams, go to http://www.microsoft.com/mcp and review the appropriate certification.

Novell, Banyan, and Sun Exemptions

The Microsoft Certified Professional program grants credit for the networking exam requirement for candidates who are certified as Novell CNEs, Master CNEs, or CNIs; Banyan CBSs or CBEs; or Sun Certified Network Administrators for Solaris 2.5 or 2.6. Go to the Microsoft Certified Professional Web site at http://www.microsoft.com/mcp for current information and details.

Other Certification Programs

In addition to the MCSE certification, Microsoft has created other certification programs that focus on specific job functions and career goals.

Microsoft Certified Systems Engineer + Internet (MCSE + I)

An individual with the MCSE + Internet credential is qualified to enhance, deploy and manage sophisticated intranet and Internet solutions that include a browser, proxy server, host servers, database, and messaging and commerce components. Microsoft Certified Systems Engineers with a specialty in the Internet are required to pass seven operating system exams and two elective exams.

Microsoft Certified Professional (MCP)

Microsoft Certified Professionals have demonstrated in-depth knowledge of at least one Microsoft product. An MCP has passed a minimum of one Microsoft operating system exam and may pass additional Microsoft Certified Professional exams to further qualify his or her skills in a particular area of specialization. A Microsoft Certified Professional has extensive knowledge about specific products but has not completed a job-function certification. The MCP credential provides a solid background for other Microsoft certifications.

Microsoft Certified Professional + Internet (MCP + I)

A person receiving the Microsoft Certified Professional + Internet certification is qualified to plan security, install and configure server products, manage server resources, extend servers to run CGI scripts or ISAPI scripts, monitor and analyze performance, and troubleshoot problems.

Microsoft Certified Professional + Site Building

Microsoft has recently created a certification designed for Web site developers. Individuals with the Microsoft Certified Professional + Site Building credential are qualified to plan, build, maintain, and manage Web sites using Microsoft technologies and products. The credential is appropriate for people who manage sophisticated, interactive Web sites that include database connectivity, multimedia, and searchable content. Microsoft Certified Professionals with a specialty in site building are required to pass two exams that measure technical proficiency and expertise.

Microsoft Certified Database Administrator (MCDBA)

The Microsoft Certified Database Administrator credential is designed for professionals who implement and administer Microsoft SQL Server databases. Microsoft Certified Database Administrators are required to pass four core exams and one elective exam.

Microsoft Certified Solution Developer (MCSD)

The Microsoft Certified Solution Developer credential is the premium certification for professionals who design and develop custom business solutions with Microsoft development tools, technologies, and platforms. The MCSD certification exams test the candidate's ability to build Web-based, distributed, and commerce applications by using Microsoft's products, such as Microsoft SQL Server, Microsoft Visual Studio, and Microsoft Transaction Server.

Certification Benefits

Obtaining Microsoft certification has many advantages. Industry professionals recognize Microsoft Certified Professionals for their knowledge and proficiency with Microsoft products and technologies. Microsoft helps to establish the program's recognition by promoting the expertise of MCPs within the industry. By becoming a Microsoft Certified Professional, you will join a worldwide community of technical professionals who have validated their expertise with Microsoft products.

In addition, you will have access to technical and product information directly from Microsoft through a secured area of the MCP Web site. You will be invited to Microsoft conferences, technical training sessions, and special events. MCPs also receive *Microsoft Certified Professional Magazine,* a career and professional development magazine.

Your organization will receive benefits when you obtain your certification. Research shows that Microsoft certification provides organizations with increased customer satisfaction and decreased support costs through improved service, increased productivity, and greater technical self-sufficiency. It also gives companies a reliable benchmark for hiring, promoting, and career planning.

Skills 2000 Program

Microsoft launched the Skills 2000 initiative to address the gap between the number of open jobs in the computing industry and the number of skilled professionals to fill them. The program, launched in 1997, builds upon the success of Microsoft's training and certification programs to reach a broader segment of the work force. Many of today's computing professionals consider the current skills gap to be their primary business challenge.

Skills 2000 aims to significantly reduce the skills gap by reaching out to individuals currently in the computing work force, as well as those interested in developing a career in information technology (IT). The program focuses on finding and placing skilled professionals in the job market today with Microsoft Solution Provider organizations. Microsoft will also facilitate internships between MSPs and students developing IT skills. In addition, Skills 2000 targets academic instructors at high schools, colleges, and universities by offering free technical training to teachers and professors who are educating the work force of tomorrow.

For more information about the Skills 2000 initiative, visit the Skills 2000 site at http://www.microsoft.com/skills2000. This site includes information about starting a career in the IT industry, IT-related articles, and a career aptitude tool.

Volunteer Technical Contributors

To volunteer for participation in one or more of the exam development phases, please sign up using the Technical Contributors online form on the MCP Web site: http://www.microsoft.com/mcp/examinfo/certsd.htm.

References

To find out more about Microsoft certification materials and programs, to register with an exam administrator, or to get other useful resources, check the following references. For Microsoft references outside the United States or Canada, contact your local Microsoft office.

Microsoft Certified Professional Program

To find information about Microsoft certification exams and information to help you prepare for any specific exam, go to http://www.microsoft.com/mcp, send e-mail to mcp@msprograms.com, or call 800-636-7544.

The MCP online magazine provides information for and about Microsoft Certified Professionals. The magazine is also a good source for exam tips. You can view the online magazine at http://www.mcpmag.com.

Microsoft Developer Network

The Microsoft Developer Network (MSDN) subscription center is your official source for software development kits, device driver kits, operating systems, and information about developing applications for Microsoft Windows and Windows NT. You can visit MSDN at http://www.microsoft.com/msdn or call 800-759-5474.

Microsoft Press

Microsoft Press offers comprehensive learning and training resources to help you get the most from Microsoft technology. For information about books published by Microsoft Press, go to http://mspress.microsoft.com or call 800-MSPRESS.

Microsoft Press ResourceLink

Microsoft Press ResourceLink is an online information resource for IT professionals who deploy, manage, or support Microsoft products and technologies. ResourceLink gives you access to the latest technical updates, tools, and utilities from Microsoft and is the most complete source of technical information about Microsoft technologies available anywhere. You can reach Microsoft Press ResourceLink at http://mspress.microsoft.com/reslink.

Microsoft TechNet IT Home

Microsoft TechNet IT Home is a resource designed for IT professionals. The Microsoft TechNet Web site is designed for anyone who evaluates, deploys, maintains, develops, or supports IT systems. Microsoft TechNet can help you stay on top of technology trends. See the TechNet Web site for more information at http://www.microsoft.com/technet/.

Microsoft Training and Certification

You can find lists of various study aids for the certification exams at http://www.microsoft.com/train_cert.

Self Test Software

Self Test Software provides the Readiness Review online assessment. For an additional fee, Self Test Software will provide test questions for this exam and other certification exams. For further information go to http://www.stsware.com/microsts.htm.

Sylvan Prometric Testing Centers

To register to take a Microsoft Certified Professional exam at any of the Sylvan Prometric testing centers around the world, go online at http://www.slspro.com. In the United States, you can call 800-755-EXAM.

Virtual University Enterprises (VUE)

You can register for a certification exam with VUE by using online registration, registering in person at a VUE testing center, or by calling 888-837-8616 in the United States. Visit http://www.vue.com/ms for testing sites, available examinations, and other registration numbers.

Glossary

add-on device A device (such as audio, networking, graphics, or SCSI controller) that is traditionally added to the base personal computer system to increase functionality.

Advanced Power Management (APM) A software interface (defined by Microsoft and Intel) between hardware-specific power management software (such as that located in a system BIOS) and an operating system power management driver.

Automatic Skip Driver Agent Automatic Skip Driver Agent identifies devices that can cause Windows 98 to stop responding (hang) when you start your computer, and then disables them so that they are bypassed when you next restart your computer. All devices or operations that have failed to start are listed by Automatic Skip Driver Agent.

backup device Any hardware component used to store data that has been backed up. This includes tape, fixed drives, or removable media such as a floppy disk or Jaz cartridge.

BIOS Basic I/O system. A set of routines that works closely with the hardware to support the transfer of information between elements of the system, such as memory, disks, and the monitor.

boot The process used by a computer when it is initially started.

Browse Master Windows 98 maintains a list of all available servers on the local network. This list, called the browse list, is maintained by a single master browser server. Additional backup browse servers can be used to minimize network traffic.

Client for NetWare Networks A network component that allows a Windows 98 computer to access Novell-based network resources. These resources include shared directories and printer queues located on a remote computer.

compression The process of reformatting files to increase available hard drive space. To compress a drive in Windows 98, you need to use Drive-Space3's Compression Agent. Only FAT16 file systems can be compressed.

cookies A means by which, under the HTTP protocol, a server or a script can maintain state or status information on the client workstation. In other words, a cookie is a collection of saved information about a person's visit to a Web page. A cookie can include such information as the way a Web page was customized or how a visitor shopped on a Web site, or it can be used to track repeat visits.

Data Link Control (DLC) A network protocol used to access special resources such as an IBM AS/400 computer or a Hewlett-Packard network printer.

DETCRASH.LOG This file records which detection steps were successfully completed so that Setup will not fail on the same step. This is a hidden file created only if the detection step caused the computer to stop responding. The file is located in the root folder of drive C.

DETLOG.TXT This file lists the start of the detection test and the test outcome. This is a hidden file located in the root folder of drive C.

Device Manager Used to check the status of current hardware device drivers. You can also remove and configure drivers using Device Manager.

DFS *See* distributed file system.

DHCP *See* Dynamic Host Configuration Protocol.

Dial-Up Networking A network component that allows Windows 98 to use a modem, or related device, to access a remote network.

Disk Defragmenter A Windows 98 utility that defragments files on a hard drive to increase the efficiency and performance of that drive. Disk Defragmenter also includes a feature to optimize the startup time of applications.

distributed file system (DFS) A file system for Windows NT Server that enables NT Server administrators to build a single, integrated directory tree that spans all the servers and shares in the corporate network.

DLC *See* Data Link Control.

DLL *See* dynamic-link library.

DMA channel A channel for direct memory access that does not involve the microprocessor, providing data transfer directly between memory and a disk drive.

docking station The base computer unit into which a user can insert a portable computer, to expand it to a desktop equivalent. A typical dock provides drive bays, expansion slots, all the ports on the desktop computer, and AC power.

domain A collection of computers that share a common domain database and security policy. Each domain has a unique name.

domain name The name by which a domain is known to the network.

Domain Name System (DNS) A protocol and system used throughout the Internet to map Internet Protocol (IP) addresses to user-friendly names such as www.microsoft.com. Sometimes referred to as the BIND service in BSD UNIX, DNS offers a static, hierarchical name service for TCP/IP hosts. DNS domains should not be confused with Windows NT networking domains.

Dr. Watson A diagnostic tool used when an application, or system component, crashes. Dr. Watson will also generate a snapshot of the current system configuration for detailed troubleshooting analysis.

DriveSpace3 A disk management utility included in Windows 98 that allows you to compress a FAT16 hard drive to increase available space.

dual boot A feature of Microsoft operating systems that allows you to boot the computer into various alternative operating systems, such as Windows 95 or Windows NT. Both operating systems are installed on the same computer.

Dynamic Host Configuration Protocol (DHCP) An industry-standard (TCP/IP) protocol that assigns Internet Protocol (IP) configurations to computers.

dynamic-link library (DLL) An API routine that user-mode applications access through ordinary procedure calls. The code for the API routine is not included in the user's executable image. Instead, the operating system automatically modifies the executable image to point to DLL procedures at run time.

ECP *See* Extended Capabilities Port.

EISA Extended Industry Standard Architecture. A 32-bit PC expansion bus designed as a superset of the ISA bus. Designed to expand the speed and data width of the legacy expansion bus while still supporting older ISA cards.

Emergency Startup Disk (ESD) A floppy disk that contains utilities required to start and troubleshoot a malfunctioning system. The startup disk loads the operating system and presents a Windows 98 command line.

Extended Capabilities Port (ECP) A port that provides high-speed printing.

FAT *See* File Allocation Table.

FAT16 An implementation of the File Allocation Table that uses larger file clusters. FAT16 is not as efficient as FAT32.

FAT32 An enhancement of the File Allocation Table that supports larger hard drives (greater than 2 GB) and uses smaller cluster sizes for better efficiency.

File Allocation Table (FAT) An area on a disk set aside to reference file locations on that disk.

File and Printer Sharing for Microsoft Networks A network component required to share local resources, such as files or printers, to Microsoft client computers.

File and Printer Sharing for NetWare Networks A network component required to share local resources, such as files or printers, to Novell NetWare clients.

File Transfer Protocol (FTP) The Internet standard high-speed protocol for downloading, or transferring, files from one computer to another. Usually this protocol is used to transfer files that are larger than those you would download through HTTP, such as files that wouldtake minutes or hours to transfer.

Firewall A system or combination of systems that enforces a boundary between two or more networks and keeps hackers out of private networks. Firewalls serve as virtual barriers to passing packets from one network to another.

FTP *See* File Transfer Protocol.

Fully Qualified Domain Name (FQDN) The combined domain name and host name, which together make up the DNS name.

gateway A computer connected to multiple physical networks, capable of routing or delivering packets between them.

group policies A tool used by administrators to centrally edit and control a computer's configuration based on the user logging in to the system.

hardware profile Different hardware configurations can be saved on the system as "hardware profiles." A user can invoke a particular hardware profile depending on his current needs. For example, laptop users may create a profile for the system when they travel and one for when they are in the office.

High Performance File System (HPFS) An OS/2 file system that allows long filenames.

host name Each computer on a network must have a unique name. The host name represents a computer's identification.

hot swap Insertion or removal of a device in the system while the device is running at full power.

HTTP *See* Hypertext Transfer Protocol.

Hypertext Transfer Protocol (HTTP) The underlying protocol by which Web clients and servers communicate. HTTP is an application-level protocol for distributed, collaborative, hypermedia information systems. It is a generic, stateless, object-oriented protocol. A feature of HTTP is the typing and negotiation of data representation, allowing systems to be built independently of the data being transferred.

IDE Integrated Device Electronics. A type of disk drive interface in which the controller electronics reside on the drive itself, eliminating the need for a separate adapter card.

Infrared Data Association (IrDA) Publisher of a wireless connectivity standard, which makes it possible to connect computers and hardware devices without using cables.

INI files Initialization files used by Windows-based applications to store per-user information that controls application startup. In Windows 98, such information is stored in the registry, and INI files are supported for backward compatibility.

Internet A set of dissimilar computer networks joined together by means of gateways that handle data transfer and the conversion of messages from the sending network to the protocols used by the receiving networks. These networks and gateways use the TCP/IP suite of protocols.

Internet Protocol (IP) The part of TCP/IP that routes messages from one Internet location to another. IP is responsible for addressing and sending TCP packets over the network.

Internetwork Packet Exchange/Sequenced Packet Exchange On Novell NetWare systems, IPX is a network layer protocol used in the file server operating system; SPX is a transport layer protocol built on top of IPX and used in client/server applications.

interrupt request (IRQ) A method by which a device can request to be serviced by the device's software driver. The system board uses a programmable interrupt controller to monitor the priority of the requests from all devices.

intranet Use of Internet standards, technologies, and products within an enterprise to function as a collaborative processing infrastructure. The term is generally used to describe the application of Internet technologies on internal corporate networks.

IO.SYS The Windows 98 version of the MS-DOS system files. IO.SYS also replaces the older CONFIG.SYS. However, if a CONFIG.SYS file exists, any entries will override IO.SYS entries.

IP address Internet Protocol address. A unique address that identifies a host on a network. It identifies a computer as a 32-bit address that is unique across a TCP/IP network.

IPX/SPX *See* Internetwork Packet Exchange/-Sequenced Packet Exchange.

IRQ *See* interrupt request.

ISDN (Integrated Services Digital Network) A completely digital telephone/telecommunications network that carries voice, data, and video information over the existing telephone network infrastructure. It is designed to provide a single interface for hooking up a telephone, fax machine, computer, and so on.

kernel The core of the layered architecture that manages the most basic operations of the operating system, such as sharing the processor between different blocks of executing code, handling hardware exceptions, and other hardware-dependent functions.

LAN Local area network. A group of computers and other devices dispersed over a relatively limited area and connected by a communications link that enables any device to interact with any other device on the network.

local printer A printer that is directly connected to one of the ports on your computer.

Microsoft Personal Web Server (PWS) A local area network Web server used to share documents in a small workgroup. It is not designed for large sites, but can be used to publish HTML files to an intranet.

Microsoft Registry Checker *See* Windows Registry Checker.

modem Modulator/demodulator. A communications tool that enables a computer to transmit information over a standard telephone line by converting digital signals to analog and vice versa.

Multiple Display Support Windows 98 can support multiple monitors to allow various views of the desktop, including multiple applications.

NDS *See* Novell Directory Services.

NetWare 3.x client software Novell's DOS-based workstation shell used by clients accessing a NetWare network.

Net Watcher This utility allows you to see who is currently using resources on your computer. You can also add shared folders and disconnect users from your computer or from specific files.

NetBEUI NetBIOS (Network Basic Input/Output System) Extended User Interface. A local area network transport protocol provided with Windows 98.

Network adapter *See* network interface card.

network interface card (NIC) A hardware card installed in a computer that so it can communicate on a network.

Network News Transfer Protocol (NNTP) The protocol used to distribute network news messages to NNTP servers and to NNTP clients (news readers) on the Internet. NNTP provides for the distribution, inquiry, retrieval, and posting of news articles by using a reliable stream-based transmission of news on the Internet.

network printer A printer that includes a NIC in order to provide direct access for network clients. No physical computer is required to host a network printer.

network protocol A set of rules and conventions by which two computers pass messages across a network. Networking software usually implements multiple levels of protocols layered one on top of another. Windows 98 includes NetBEUI, TCP/IP, and IPX/SPX protocols.

NIC *See* network interface card.

Novell Directory Services Novell's network database that contains information about user accounts and available resources. NDS allows users and developers access to network resources via an object model represented in a hierarchical tree.

NTFS *See* Windows NT file system.

OnNow A design initiative that seeks to create all the components required for a comprehensive, system-wide approach to system and device power control. OnNow is a term for a PC that is always on but appears off and that responds immediately to user or other requests.

partition A portion of a physical disk that functions as though it were a physically separate unit. With Fdisk, you may divide a disk into two main components, primary partition and extended partition. After formatting, the primary partition is your C drive. The extended partition may be divided into smaller drives, such as D, E, F, and so on.

PCI Peripheral Component Interconnect. A high-performance, 32-bit or 64-bit bus designed to be used with devices that have high bandwidth requirements, such as display subsystems.

PDC *See* Primary Domain Controller.

peer-to-peer network Sometimes called a workgroup, a peer-to-peer network does not include a server to authenticate user logins. Each computer maintains its own user database. Network resources are controlled using share-level security (resources are password-protected for Read-only and Full access).

PING A DOS-based TCP/IP utility that can verify a remote computer can be "seen" on the network and verify general network performance capability between the local and remote computers.

Plug and Play A design philosophy and set of specifications that describe hardware and software changes to the PC and its peripherals, making it possible to add new components without having to perform technical procedures.

Point-to-Point Protocol An industry standard, a part of Windows 98 Dial-Up Networking, designed to ensure interoperability with remote access software from other vendors. It is used in making point-to-point links, especially with dial-up modem servers.

Point-to-Point Tunneling Protocol Protocol that enables a computer to securely connect to the Internet or an intranet by tunneling through an Internet or LAN connection.

PPP *See* Point-to-Point Protocol.

PPTP *See* Point-to-Point Tunneling Protocol.

Primary Domain Controller (PDC) The first computer named in a Windows NT Server domain during installation. It contains a master copy of domain information, validates users, and can act as file, print, and application server. Every Windows NT domain is required to have one, and only one, primary domain controller.

proxy server A server that acts as a go-between, converting information from Web servers into HTML to be delivered to a client computer. It also provides a way to deliver network services to computers on a secure subnet without those computers needing to have direct access to the World Wide Web.

registry The database repository for information about a computer's configuration. The registry supersedes the use of separate INI files for all system components and applications that know how to store values in the registry.

Registry Checker *See* Windows Registry Checker.

Registry Editor An application, provided with Windows 98, that is used to view and edit entries in the registry.

Remote Access Service (RAS) A service that provides remote networking for telecommuters, mobile workers, and system administrators who monitor and manage servers at multiple branch offices.

removable device Any hardware device, or media, that can be "unplugged" from a computer without requiring the computer to be physically opened. Examples include a floppy disk or a removable disk (such as a Jaz cartridge).

Resource Meter Resource Meter monitors the system resources your programs are using.

roaming users Roaming users are users who can log on to any computer system they require for their work. This might be on a day-to-day basis when the user arrives at work or if the user moves to different locations in a building and does not necessarily have a dedicated office computer.

routing The process of transferring packets from one network segment to another.

SCSI Small Computer Standard Interface. An I/O bus designed as a method for connecting several classes of peripherals to a host system without requiring modifications to generic hardware and software.

Serial Line Internet Protocol (SLIP) An older industry standard that allows remote access for Internet connections. It is now generally replaced by Point-to-Point Protocol (PPP).

Server Message Block (SMB) The protocol developed by Microsoft, Intel, and IBM that defines a series of commands used to pass information between network computers. The redirector packages SMB requests into a network control block (NCB) structure that can be sent over the network to a remote device. The network provider listens for SMB messages destined for it and removes the data portion of the SMB request so that it can be processed by a local device.

setup script An ASCII text file used by the Setup application to standardize and automate the installation process.

SETUPLOG.TXT This file records what took place during Setup, including successes and failures. It is used by Safe Recovery to determine where Setup should resume. The file is located in the root folder of drive C.

share-level access *See* share-level security.

share-level security A password-protected security scheme that assigns a password for each shared resource. Access to the resource is granted when the user enters the appropriate password. This is a simple security method that is not as secure as user-level security.

shared resource Any device, data, or program that is used by more than one other device or program. For Windows 98, refers to any resource that is made available to network users, such as directories, files, printers, and named pipes.

SLIP *See* Serial Line Internet Protocol.

SMB *See* Server Message Block.

System Configuration Utility Automates routine Windows troubleshooting steps. This tool allows you to modify the system configuration by using check boxes. It also allows you to troubleshoot problems through a process of elimination using check boxes.

System File Checker This Windows 98 tool verifies the integrity of system files. It scans the system for changed, deleted, or corrupt files and can extract original Windows 98 versions.

System Information Utility This Windows 98 tool, also called MSInfo, displays information such as hardware resources, devices installed, and corresponding device drivers. You can also use this utility to diagnose and solve computer problems. MSInfo can be used to view reports generated on a remote computer.

System Monitor A Windows 98 tool used to help determine the cause of a problem on a local or remote computer. It does this by measuring the performance of hardware, software services, and applications. When you make a change to the system configuration, System Monitor shows the effect of your changes on overall system performance.

system policies Optional configuration files that can be used to override any settings contained in the registry. System policies can contain additional data specific to the network or corporate environment, as established by a network administrator. These policies are contained in the CONFIG.POL file.

TCP/IP *See* Transmission Control Protocol/Internet Protocol.

TRACERT A DOS-based TCP/IP utility that provides detailed information about the route used to access remote computers via the local intranet or the public Internet.

Transmission Control Protocol/Internet Protocol A networking protocol that allows computers to communicate across interconnected networks and the Internet. Every computer on the Internet supports TCP/IP.

UDP *See* User Datagram Protocol.

Universal Resource Locator (URL) A naming convention that uniquely identifies the location of a computer, directory, or file on the Internet. The URL also specifies the appropriate Internet protocol, such as HTTP or FTP.

Universal Serial Bus (USB) A bidirectional, isochronous, dynamically attachable serial interface for adding peripheral devices such as game controllers, serial and parallel ports, and input devices on a single bus.

URL *See* Universal Resource Locator.

USB *See* Universal Serial Bus.

User Datagram Protocol (UDP) A TCP/IP connectionless mode protocol describing how transmitted messages reach application programs within a destination computer. It is more primitive than TCP and does not guarantee that the packet being sent across the network arrives at its destination.

user profile Windows 98 allows for multiple users to log on to the computer locally. Each user can configure the system—for example, by changing desktop themes or screen resolution—based on his or her individual preferences. These configurations can then be saved as a user profile and recalled for automatic use the next time the user logs on to the computer.

user-level access *See* user-level security.

user-level security When you're using a security provider, such as Windows NT Server, access to network resources is granted on a per-user basis. Both individual user names and groups of users can be given Read-only or Full access to a network resource. Access is based on a validated user login.

Version Conflict Manager Sometimes, when installing software, you may have a newer version of a file on your system than the one being installed. Windows 98 Setup automatically installs the Windows 98 file over the newer file and stores the newer version of the file in the \Windows\VCM folder. Those files can be viewed or restored with Version Conflict Manger.

Virtual Loadable Module (VLM) A Novell network client architecture that uses packet burst technology. VLM can be used to allow Windows 98 clients access to Novell servers.

virtual private network (VPN) A VPN is a remote LAN that can be accessed through the Internet by using the PPTP, or other protocols.

VLM *See* Virtual Loadable Module.

VPN *See* virtual private network.

Windows NT file system (NTFS) The file system designed for use specifically with the Windows NT operating system. NTFS supports file system recovery and extremely large storage media, in addition to other advantages. It also supports object-oriented applications by treating all files as objects with user-defined and system-defined attributes.

Windows Registry Checker A Windows 98 utility that allows you to check the current state of the registry and manually back up the registry.

Windows Report Tool A Web-based reporting tool that gathers system information and uploads it using HTTP to a support provider. The report includes a snapshot of the system in Microsoft System Information's format.

Winipcfg A Windows 98 utility that provides detailed information about the current TCP/IP settings. This tool can also be used to refresh DHCP settings.

workgroup In a peer-to-peer network, a workgroup groups computers together to provide access to one another's resources. Computers in a workgroup are listed in Network Neighborhood. Only share-level security can be implemented when a workgroup environment is used.

Index

Microsoft Press Resource Kits—
powerhouse resources to minimize costs
while maximizing performance

**Microsoft® Windows NT® Server 4.0
Resource Kit**
ISBN   1-57231-344-7
U.S.A. $149.95
U.K.   £140.99 [V.A.T. included]
Canada $199.95

**Microsoft Windows NT Workstation 4.0
Resource Kit**
ISBN   1-57231-343-9
U.S.A. $69.95
U.K.   £64.99 [V.A.T. included]
Canada $94.95

**Microsoft Internet Information
Server Resource Kit**
ISBN   1-57231-638-1
U.S.A. $49.99
U.K.   £46.99 [V.A.T. included]
Canada $71.99

**Microsoft Windows® 98
Resource Kit**
ISBN   1-57231-644-6
U.S.A. $69.99
U.K.   £64.99 [V.A.T. included]
Canada $100.99

**Microsoft Internet Explorer
Resource Kit**
ISBN   1-57231-842-2
U.S.A. $49.99
U.K.   £46.99 [V.A.T. included]
Canada $71.99

Direct from the Microsoft
product groups, the resources
packed into these bestselling
kits meet the demand for
hardcore use-now tools
and information for the IT
professional. Each kit contains
precise technical reference,
essential utilities, installation
and rollout tactics, planning
guides, and upgrade strategies.
Use them to save time, reduce
cost of ownership, and maximize
your organization's technology
investment.

mspress.microsoft.com

**Microsoft BackOffice® Resource Kit,
Second Edition**
ISBN   1-57231-632-2
U.S.A. $199.99
U.K.   £187.99 [V.A.T. included]
Canada $289.99

Microsoft Press® products are available worldwide wherever quality
computer books are sold. For more information, contact your book or
computer retailer, software reseller, or local Microsoft Sales Office, or
visit our Web site at mspress.microsoft.com. To locate your nearest
source for Microsoft Press products, or to order directly, call 1-800-
MSPRESS in the U.S. (in Canada, call 1-800-268-2222).

Prices and availability dates are subject to change.

http://mspress.microsoft.com/reslink/

ResourceLink—your online IT library!

Access the full line of Microsoft Press® Resource Kits for the Windows® and BackOffice® families, along with MCSE Training Kits and other IT-specific resources at <u>mspress.microsoft.com/reslink/</u>. Microsoft Press ResourceLink is the essential online information service for IT professionals. Get the latest technical updates, support alerts, insider tips, and downloadable utilities—direct from Microsoft. If you evaluate, deploy, or support Microsoft® technologies and products, the information you need to optimize their performance—and your own—is online and ready for work at ResourceLink.

For a complimentary 30-day trial CD packed with Microsoft Press
IT products, order through our Web site: <u>mspress.microsoft.com/reslink/</u>

MICROSOFT LICENSE AGREEMENT

Book Companion CD

IMPORTANT—READ CAREFULLY: This Microsoft End-User License Agreement ("EULA") is a legal agreement between you (either an individual or an entity) and Microsoft Corporation for the Microsoft product identified above, which includes computer software and may include associated media, printed materials, and "online" or electronic documentation ("SOFTWARE PRODUCT"). Any component included within the SOFTWARE PRODUCT that is accompanied by a separate End-User License Agreement shall be governed by such agreement and not the terms set forth below. By installing, copying, or otherwise using the SOFTWARE PRODUCT, you agree to be bound by the terms of this EULA. If you do not agree to the terms of this EULA, you are not authorized to install, copy, or otherwise use the SOFTWARE PRODUCT; you may, however, return the SOFTWARE PRODUCT, along with all printed materials and other items that form a part of the Microsoft product that includes the SOFTWARE PRODUCT, to the place you obtained them for a full refund.

SOFTWARE PRODUCT LICENSE

The SOFTWARE PRODUCT is protected by United States copyright laws and international copyright treaties, as well as other intellectual property laws and treaties. The SOFTWARE PRODUCT is licensed, not sold.

1. **GRANT OF LICENSE.** This EULA grants you the following rights:

    a. **Software Product.** You may install and use one copy of the SOFTWARE PRODUCT on a single computer. The primary user of the computer on which the SOFTWARE PRODUCT is installed may make a second copy for his or her exclusive use on a portable computer.

    b. **Storage/Network Use.** You may also store or install a copy of the SOFTWARE PRODUCT on a storage device, such as a network server, used only to install or run the SOFTWARE PRODUCT on your other computers over an internal network; however, you must acquire and dedicate a license for each separate computer on which the SOFTWARE PRODUCT is installed or run from the storage device. A license for the SOFTWARE PRODUCT may not be shared or used concurrently on different computers.

    c. **License Pak.** If you have acquired this EULA in a Microsoft License Pak, you may make the number of additional copies of the computer software portion of the SOFTWARE PRODUCT authorized on the printed copy of this EULA, and you may use each copy in the manner specified above. You are also entitled to make a corresponding number of secondary copies for portable computer use as specified above.

    d. **Sample Code.** Solely with respect to portions, if any, of the SOFTWARE PRODUCT that are identified within the SOFTWARE PRODUCT as sample code (the "SAMPLE CODE"):

    i. **Use and Modification.** Microsoft grants you the right to use and modify the source code version of the SAMPLE CODE, *provided* you comply with subsection (d)(iii) below. You may not distribute the SAMPLE CODE, or any modified version of the SAMPLE CODE, in source code form.

    ii. **Redistributable Files.** Provided you comply with subsection (d)(iii) below, Microsoft grants you a nonexclusive, royalty-free right to reproduce and distribute the object code version of the SAMPLE CODE and of any modified SAMPLE CODE, other than SAMPLE CODE, or any modified version thereof, designated as not redistributable in the Readme file that forms a part of the SOFTWARE PRODUCT (the "Non-Redistributable Sample Code"). All SAMPLE CODE other than the Non-Redistributable Sample Code is collectively referred to as the "REDISTRIBUTABLES."

    iii. **Redistribution Requirements.** If you redistribute the REDISTRIBUTABLES, you agree to: (i) distribute the REDISTRIBUTABLES in object code form only in conjunction with and as a part of your software application product; (ii) not use Microsoft's name, logo, or trademarks to market your software application product; (iii) include a valid copyright notice on your software application product; (iv) indemnify, hold harmless, and defend Microsoft from and against any claims or lawsuits, including attorney's fees, that arise or result from the use or distribution of your software application product; and (v) not permit further distribution of the REDISTRIBUTABLES by your end user. Contact Microsoft for the applicable royalties due and other licensing terms for all other uses and/or distribution of the REDISTRIBUTABLES.

2. **DESCRIPTION OF OTHER RIGHTS AND LIMITATIONS.**

    - **Limitations on Reverse Engineering, Decompilation, and Disassembly.** You may not reverse engineer, decompile, or disassemble the SOFTWARE PRODUCT, except and only to the extent that such activity is expressly permitted by applicable law notwithstanding this limitation.

    - **Separation of Components.** The SOFTWARE PRODUCT is licensed as a single product. Its component parts may not be separated for use on more than one computer.

    - **Rental.** You may not rent, lease, or lend the SOFTWARE PRODUCT.

- **Support Services.** Microsoft may, but is not obligated to, provide you with support services related to the SOFTWARE PRODUCT ("Support Services"). Use of Support Services is governed by the Microsoft policies and programs described in the user manual, in "online" documentation, and/or other Microsoft-provided materials. Any supplemental software code provided to you as part of the Support Services shall be considered part of the SOFTWARE PRODUCT and subject to the terms and conditions of this EULA. With respect to technical information you provide to Microsoft as part of the Support Services, Microsoft may use such information for its business purposes, including for product support and development. Microsoft will not utilize such technical information in a form that personally identifies you.

- **Software Transfer.** You may permanently transfer all of your rights under this EULA, provided you retain no copies, you transfer all of the SOFTWARE PRODUCT (including all component parts, the media and printed materials, any upgrades, this EULA, and, if applicable, the Certificate of Authenticity), **and** the recipient agrees to the terms of this EULA.

- **Termination.** Without prejudice to any other rights, Microsoft may terminate this EULA if you fail to comply with the terms and conditions of this EULA. In such event, you must destroy all copies of the SOFTWARE PRODUCT and all of its component parts.

3. **COPYRIGHT.** All title and copyrights in and to the SOFTWARE PRODUCT (including but not limited to any images, photographs, animations, video, audio, music, text, SAMPLE CODE, REDISTRIBUTABLES, and "applets" incorporated into the SOFTWARE PRODUCT) and any copies of the SOFTWARE PRODUCT are owned by Microsoft or its suppliers. The SOFT-WARE PRODUCT is protected by copyright laws and international treaty provisions. Therefore, you must treat the SOFTWARE PRODUCT like any other copyrighted material **except** that you may install the SOFTWARE PRODUCT on a single computer provided you keep the original solely for backup or archival purposes. You may not copy the printed materials accompanying the SOFTWARE PRODUCT.

4. **U.S. GOVERNMENT RESTRICTED RIGHTS.** The SOFTWARE PRODUCT and documentation are provided with RESTRICTED RIGHTS. Use, duplication, or disclosure by the Government is subject to restrictions as set forth in subparagraph (c)(1)(ii) of the Rights in Technical Data and Computer Software clause at DFARS 252.227-7013 or subparagraphs (c)(1) and (2) of the Commercial Computer Software—Restricted Rights at 48 CFR 52.227-19, as applicable. Manufacturer is Microsoft Corporation/One Microsoft Way/Redmond, WA 98052-6399.

5. **EXPORT RESTRICTIONS.** You agree that you will not export or re-export the SOFTWARE PRODUCT, any part thereof, or any process or service that is the direct product of the SOFTWARE PRODUCT (the foregoing collectively referred to as the "Restricted Components"), to any country, person, entity, or end user subject to U.S. export restrictions. You specifically agree not to export or re-export any of the Restricted Components (i) to any country to which the U.S. has embargoed or restricted the export of goods or services, which currently include, but are not necessarily limited to Cuba, Iran, Iraq, Libya, North Korea, Sudan, and Syria, or to any national of any such country, wherever located, who intends to transmit or transport the Restricted Components back to such country; (ii) to any end-user who you know or have reason to know will utilize the Restricted Components in the design, development, or production of nuclear, chemical, or biological weapons; or (iii) to any end-user who has been prohibited from participating in U.S. export transactions by any federal agency of the U.S. government. You warrant and represent that neither the BXA nor any other U.S. federal agency has suspended, revoked, or denied your export privileges.

DISCLAIMER OF WARRANTY

NO WARRANTIES OR CONDITIONS. MICROSOFT EXPRESSLY DISCLAIMS ANY WARRANTY OR CONDITION FOR THE SOFTWARE PRODUCT. THE SOFTWARE PRODUCT AND ANY RELATED DOCUMENTATION IS PROVIDED "AS IS" WITHOUT WARRANTY OR CONDITION OF ANY KIND, EITHER EXPRESS OR IMPLIED, INCLUDING, WITHOUT LIMITA-TION, THE IMPLIED WARRANTIES OF MERCHANTABILITY, FITNESS FOR A PARTICULAR PURPOSE, OR NONINFRINGEMENT. THE ENTIRE RISK ARISING OUT OF USE OR PERFORMANCE OF THE SOFTWARE PRODUCT REMAINS WITH YOU.

LIMITATION OF LIABILITY. TO THE MAXIMUM EXTENT PERMITTED BY APPLICABLE LAW, IN NO EVENT SHALL MICROSOFT OR ITS SUPPLIERS BE LIABLE FOR ANY SPECIAL, INCIDENTAL, INDIRECT, OR CONSEQUENTIAL DAM-AGES WHATSOEVER (INCLUDING, WITHOUT LIMITATION, DAMAGES FOR LOSS OF BUSINESS PROFITS, BUSINESS INTERRUPTION, LOSS OF BUSINESS INFORMATION, OR ANY OTHER PECUNIARY LOSS) ARISING OUT OF THE USE OF OR INABILITY TO USE THE SOFTWARE PRODUCT OR THE PROVISION OF OR FAILURE TO PROVIDE SUPPORT SERVICES, EVEN IF MICROSOFT HAS BEEN ADVISED OF THE POSSIBILITY OF SUCH DAMAGES. IN ANY CASE, MICROSOFT'S ENTIRE LIABILITY UNDER ANY PROVISION OF THIS EULA SHALL BE LIMITED TO THE GREATER OF THE AMOUNT ACTUALLY PAID BY YOU FOR THE SOFTWARE PRODUCT OR US$5.00; PROVIDED HOWEVER, IF YOU HAVE ENTERED INTO A MICROSOFT SUPPORT SERVICES AGREEMENT, MICROSOFT'S ENTIRE LIABILITY REGARDING SUPPORT SERVICES SHALL BE GOVERNED BY THE TERMS OF THAT AGREEMENT. BECAUSE SOME STATES AND JURISDICTIONS DO NOT ALLOW THE EXCLUSION OR LIMITATION OF LIABILITY, THE ABOVE LIMITATION MAY NOT APPLY TO YOU.

MISCELLANEOUS

This EULA is governed by the laws of the State of Washington USA, except and only to the extent that applicable law mandates governing law of a different jurisdiction.

Should you have any questions concerning this EULA, or if you desire to contact Microsoft for any reason, please contact the Microsoft subsidiary serving your country, or write: Microsoft Sales Information Center/One Microsoft Way/Redmond, WA 98052-6399.

System Requirements

To use the Readiness Review compact disc, you need a computer equipped with the following minimum configuration:

- 486 or higher Intel-based processor (486 must be running in Enhanced mode).

- Microsoft Windows 95, Windows 98, Windows NT 4.0 or later.

- 4 MB of RAM.

- 15 MB of available disk space.

- CD-ROM drive.

- Mouse or other pointing device (recommended).

Register Today!

Return this
*MCSE Readiness Review – Exam 70-098:
Implementing and Supporting Microsoft® Windows® 98*
registration card today

Microsoft®Press
mspress.microsoft.com

0-7356-0671-4

MCSE Readiness Review – Exam 70-098:
Implementing and Supporting Microsoft® Windows® 98

_____ _____ _____
FIRST NAME   MIDDLE INITIAL   LAST NAME

_____
INSTITUTION OR COMPANY NAME

_____
ADDRESS

_____

_____ _____ _____
CITY   STATE   ZIP

                                                            (   )
_____
E-MAIL ADDRESS   PHONE NUMBER

U.S. and Canada addresses only. Fill in information above and mail postage-free.
Please mail only the bottom half of this page.

*For information about Microsoft Press®
products, visit our Web site at*
mspress.microsoft.com

Microsoft®*Press*